The Gothic Tarot Compendium

A detailed guide to understanding and using
The Gothic Tarot

Illustrated by Joseph Vargo
Written by Joseph Vargo and Joseph Iorillo
Book Designed by Christine Filipak

Monolith Graphics
Cleveland, Ohio, USA
www.MonolithGraphics.com

PUBLISHED BY MONOLITH GRAPHICS
CLEVELAND, OHIO, USA
WWW.MONOLITHGRAPHICS.COM

Cover and Interior Artwork by Joseph Vargo

Publisher's Cataloging-in-Publication Data
The Gothic Tarot Compendium
by Joseph Vargo and Joseph Iorillo
ISBN: 0-9788857-2-4
ISBN(13): 978-0-9788857-2-4
1. non-fiction, divination, tarot
2. Vargo, Joseph

Made in the USA

CONTENTS

A HISTORY OF THE TAROT 4
THE GOTHIC TAROT 8

THE MAJOR ARCANA 11

THE MINOR ARCANA 101

A History of the Tarot

The word "Tarot" is of uncertain origin, although some historians believe it is derived from the Hebrew word "torah," which means "the law." Other theories link the name to the Taro River in northern Italy or to the Egyptian word "tarosh," which means "the royal way."

The Tarot deck itself has a similarly murky lineage. An eighteenth-century French scholar and Freemason named Antoine Court de Gebelin claimed the cards originated in ancient Egypt and were used to introduce initiates into the secrets of the Egyptian priesthood. Gebelin believed that the deck's Major Arcana illustrated secrets from the Egyptian Book of Thoth, a legendary lost tome thought to contain spiritual knowledge of the highest order. Other Tarot enthusiasts likewise claimed the deck came from Egypt. A French philosopher and physician named Papus insisted the Tarot represented images and designs found in hidden chambers below the Pyramids; these images detailed rites of initiation into Egyptian mysticism. According to Papus, the decks were created in order to preserve the details of these rites in the event the Pyramids were plundered or destroyed.

There is no definitive archaeological evidence that ties the Tarot to ancient Egypt, nor is there evidence for any of the other theories that subsequently emerged regarding the Tarot's origin. For example, a noted nineteenth-century Frenchman and prominent occultist, Alphonse Louis Constant, claimed the cards were ancient Hebrew methods of instructing people in the branch of Jewish mysticism known as Kabbalah. Among other claims, Constant believed the 22 cards of the Major Arcana represented the letters of the Hebrew alphabet. Another theory suggested the Tarot came from Morocco in the eleventh century as a sort of database encoded with much of the knowledge from the famous libraries destroyed in Alexandria, Egypt. The Tarot has also been believed to be a pictorial record of Asian Indian holy writings, as well as a record of the esoteric knowledge held by ancient alchemists and the Knights Templar, the twelfth century secret society of Christian monks that was ultimately persecuted by the Catholic Church.

While no real evidence has been found to explain the birth of the Tarot, the first documented reference to the cards occurred in Italy in the fifteenth century. This reference took the form of a sermon by a Franciscan friar condemning the Tarot as an invention of Satan. The friar claimed that the cards of the Major Arcana, which were used as the basis of a card game played by the nobility, were heretical, and those who played the game were surrendering their souls to the Devil. Interestingly, the sermon did not mention the cards' use in divination, leading some historians to believe that the Tarot was not used for fortune telling until centuries later.

The use of the Tarot as a means to predict a person's future began in the late 1700s, when the occultist Jean-Baptiste Alliette, also known as Etteilla, published a collection of divinatory meanings for Tarot cards, as well as ordinary playing cards. Coinciding with Antoine Court de Gebelin's claims that the Tarot represented ancient mystical knowledge from Egypt, Etteilla's formalized explanations of the cards spurred renewed interest in the Tarot, and the cards soon became one of the most popular and easily available means of supposedly glimpsing the future.

In addition to its divinatory use, the Tarot is seen by some scholars as a symbolic account of the themes embedded within the legends of the Holy Grail that began circulating in the twelfth century. In the Grail stories, knights such as Percival pass through various stages of initiation and maturation in order to obtain a much-desired object called the Grail, which has been defined as a plate or dish or cup, depending upon the story. This Grail has the power of restoring health, creating food and abundance, and healing lands blighted by famine or strife. Although later versions of the Grail legends were used by the Christian Church and rewritten in order to associate the Grail with the cup used by Jesus at the Last Supper, the original Grail stories were not Christian. In fact, many scholars have seen a distinctly pagan or Eastern philosophic aura in the legends, particularly in their recurring ideas of cyclic renewal and the harmony between a person's male and female aspects.

Many portions of the Grail stories appear in symbolic form in the Tarot deck. For example, the swords, spears, dishes and chalices that play prominent roles in the Grail legends show up in the Minor Arcana as swords, wands, pentacles and cups. The pagan-influenced Grail stories are subliminal criticisms of Church orthodoxy, which stresses such unhealthy practices as sexual repression, subjugation of women and avoidance of the supposedly evil forces of the natural world.

The earliest known Tarot cards appeared in Italy from the early to mid 1400s. Known as Tarocchi, these cards were hand-painted, although other specimens from around this time are printed cards of inferior quality. It was not until several hundred years later, however, that more elaborate and well-known Tarot decks were created.

During the 16th century, the Tarot de Marseilles became the standard deck throughout Europe. This traditional deck got its name from the city of Marseilles, France because it was manufactured there in the 17th and 18th centuries. During this time period there were several incarnations of the Marseille deck, the most famous being those designed by Nicholas Conver in 1760. The Major Arcana of the Marseille deck is the most enduring and influential of all Tarot designs. The Marseille Tarot became popular among the French occultists, who began using them primarily for mystical divination purposes. Soon afterward, the use of Tarot cards by fortune-tellers became widespread throughout Europe.

In the late 1800s, Tarot cards underwent a radical change when Alfred Edward Waite, an occult philosopher and member of several secret societies, including the Hermetic Order of the Golden Dawn, commissioned an artist named Pamela Coleman-Smith to create what he hoped would become the definitive Tarot. This deck became the Rider-Waite deck, which is the most widely used deck today. Waite's vision was to create a deck of esoteric images that would help the reader to fully understand the specific divinatory meaning of each card. The Rider-Waite deck was the first incarnation of the Tarot to use elaborate artistic depictions for the cards of the Minor Arcana rather than simple designs or motifs. In accordance with the beliefs of the Golden Dawn, Waite also swapped the positions of the Strength and Justice cards to make them correspond with the Kabbalah, making Strength number 8 and Justice number 11.

In the early twentieth century, the infamous occult figure Aleister Crowley wrote The Book of Thoth, which revealed his unique vision of the Tarot. Years later, he worked closely with an artist named Lady Frieda Harris to bring the Thoth Tarot to life. A believer in Egyptian mysticism, Crowley imbued his deck with distinctly Egyptian symbols and themes, and Lady Frieda's vibrant and surreal artwork added a new age appeal to the cards.

Other popular Tarot decks have appeared in recent years, some of them serving as showcases for the works of notable fantasy artists. Several of these popular modern decks have been created around motifs utilizing dragons, angels, fairies, and various other mythological deities and creatures, although many of these decks have strayed from the original conceptions of the Tarot and are referred to as "oracle decks."

Unlike the majority of modern decks, which use art that bears little or no relation to the traditional symbolism of the individual cards, the Gothic Tarot involved the meticulous adaptation of Joseph Vargo's art to fit the traditional Tarot symbols and meanings. Because of this close attention to detail, the Gothic Tarot has become an extremely popular and respected deck among serious Tarot readers worldwide.

For centuries, Tarot cards have created controversy wherever they have appeared. Many of their strange images speak deeply to those who read them, allowing the cards to be interpreted on a very personal level. Whether seen as an oracle of divine wisdom, a window into the future or an accumulation of ancient mystical knowledge, the Tarot deck is an undeniably fascinating cipher that serves as a guide for those who search for the answers to life's mysteries.

THE GOTHIC TAROT

Born of the night, they lurk in the shadows—
Gargoyles of living stone, lost souls who wander mist-shrouded
cemeteries, and vampires who dwell in forbidden crypts.

The Gothic Tarot was created in 2002 by renowned gothic fantasy artist Joseph Vargo. A dark oracle consisting of all 78 cards of the Major and Minor Arcana, this lavish deck is adorned with images of vampires, ghosts, gargoyles, dark angels and other creatures of the night. Vargo's interest in ancient mysticism and symbolism inspired him throughout his artistic career and acted as the impetus that motivated him to undertake the project.

With a body of work including more than 300 original paintings and renderings, Vargo utilized much of his existing art in the creation of the Gothic Tarot, in some cases changing his designs to fit the specifications of the individual card. In certain instances the art needed no alteration whatsoever. Vargo was struck by the serendipity of how some older images fell perfectly into place, as if they were always meant to represent precise Tarot concepts. He also created several new works of art specifically for the deck. Although the project took less than one year to complete, the Gothic Tarot represents over ten years of the artist's career.

Aside from its prophetic and divinitaory value, the Tarot is also an art form unto itself that reflects upon the culture and style of the era while appealing to varying personal tastes. After studying several of the most popular Tarot decks and researching numerous older cards, Vargo went to great lengths to create an artistic deck that was both cohesive and aesthetically pleasing. Building upon much of the familiar iconography established by these earlier decks, the artist put his own personal gothic flair on traditional symbolism. The resulting deck has won the praise of Tarot experts worldwide.

The gothic realm is populated with mysterious, brooding and provocative denizens of the shadows. In Vargo's artistic frame of reference, the forces of darkness are personified by seductive undead creatures, while the forces of light are depicted as fierce warrior angels and beautiful wandering spirits. In his art book, *Born of the Night: The Gothic Fantasy Art of Joseph Vargo*, the artist revealed the stories behind many of his popular works. Although he described many of his paintings, Vargo's commentary mainly focused on the art and history and did not delve into the details of the occult symbolism that the images contain.

Heeding the call to create a guidebook for the Gothic Tarot, Vargo set out to explain the meaning and specific symbolism of the cards of his deck. His extensive research into the esoteric origins, history and evolution of the Tarot bring an enlightened understanding of Old World concepts and symbolism, allowing these mystical and occult factors to be easily translated and fully comprehended by a contemporary audience.

Beyond its concise symbolic explanations, this compendium also allows readers to utilize the Gothic Tarot to its fullest divinitory potential by offering detailed instructions regarding several traditional and original card layouts that reinforce the gothic theme of the artwork. The Gothic Tarot can be a useful tool that helps to guide us on our life's path, lending positive reinforcement in regard to questionable matters and warning us of potentially dangerous risks that may lie in wait. With this in-depth key to understanding the cards, Tarot readers can offer insightful advice as to how to attain the best outcome in any situation.

While the Gothic Tarot stands as a major achievement in fantasy art, its meticulous attention to detail and divinatory symbolism have made it an important milestone in the history of the Tarot as well. Vargo's captivating imagery creates a seductive gothic lens through which we can view our spiritual evolution, enabling us to focus our mind's eye upon our past experiences, our present accomplishments and perhaps our ultimate destiny.

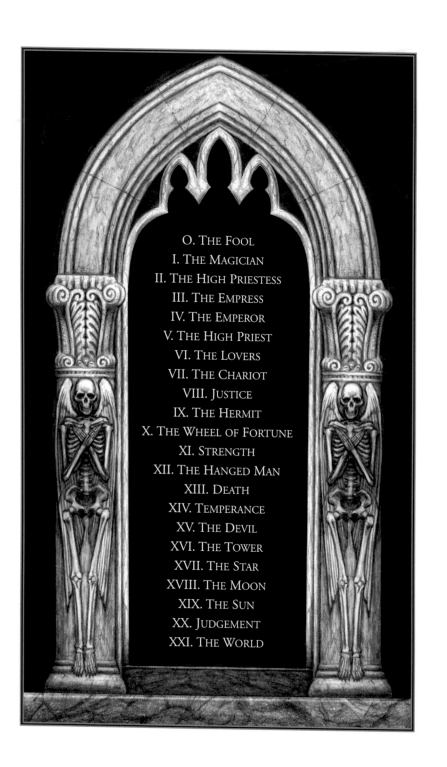

THE MAJOR ARCANA

The Major Arcana consists of 22 cards that represent archetypes of people, physical, emotional and spiritual states, virtues, vices and possible destinies. Certain cards may symbolize an actual person or a personality trait. The Major Arcana also represents one's journey though life or a particular circumstance. The Fool traditionally depicts one who is just starting out on the journey and the World is the time or place where that journey comes to its completion.

The cards are interpreted according to their position in the spread and the outlook of the individual being read. What one person may consider to be an obstacle may appear as a challenge to others. The cards also hold separate meanings, sometimes to the contrary, when they appear reversed or inverted.

The Major Arcana is comprised of three specific subcategories, each consisting of seven cards. The first set, which encompasses cards 1 through 7, are symbols of the material world. The next set, consisting of cards 8 through 14, are symbols of the intuitive mind. The final set, cards 15 through 21, constitute the realm of change. The Fool, representing an innocent person starting on life's journey, was not originally designated with a number, although in modern decks, it is often labeled with the number 0.

O

THE FOOL

O. THE FOOL

The beginning of a journey, delving heedlessly into the unknown, a leap of faith, a folly, one who is naïve, or seeking experience. Reversed: Unsure, careless, neglectful, vane, apathetic.

Divinatory meaning: You are on the threshold of a mysterious new stage in your life. You will traverse unfamiliar territory, but do not lose sight of your goal. Look to the lessons you have learned from past experiences to help you overcome future obstacles. A sense of solitude or self-reliance may pervade as you enter into this new venture, but you are not alone. A companion lends support and accompanies you during this time, offering guidance when needed; however, the path you take will ultimately be one of your own choosing. The Fool represents the seeker of wisdom who gains knowledge from everything that surrounds him, so remember that even the most difficult times can teach valuable lessons. If this card is reversed, it denotes insecurity, carelessness and lack of focus on your goal.

A cloaked wraith ascends five steps leading to an ancient archway, beyond which lies a mysterious and shadowy domain. The figure wears an expressionless mask, covering the traveler's true demeanor. A large black wolf steps forward from the darkness and three ravens are perched above the crumbling stone arch. In the background, a solitary light illuminates a tower window.

The Fool card represents a seeker of wisdom who looks to the Tarot for guidance. Traditionally, the main character is depicted as a harlequin, festively adorned in brightly colored clothes; however, Vargo represents the Fool as a dark spirit wearing a plain theatrical mask, capturing the essence of both the spiritual self and the physical facade.

The specter symbolically exists at the crossroads between the realm of the living and the dead, and the archway, which Vargo describes as a portal, represents the threshold between a familiar realm and the mysterious domain that lies ahead. The tower light in the distance signifies a beacon to guide the traveler through the gloom. The unknown future lies before us and the traveler can either remain focused on his goal and follow the clear path to illumination, or become lost in the surrounding darkness.

The wolf companion at the traveler's side hearkens to the customary representation of the Fool's dog; however, his demeanor is a departure from the traditional depictions that show a carefree pup frolicking at his master's feet. Here, the wolf is aware of his surroundings, keeping a protective eye on any dangers that may threaten his master. Representing a wild spirit, both cunning and formidable, the wolf acts as a guardian and loyal companion.

Overhead, three large ravens sit perched atop the stone arch, their eyes glowing red, their ebony wings barely visible against the black of night. Often portrayed in many of Vargo's works, ravens indicate brooding spirits, magical familiars and ominous creatures of the shadows who foretell of darkness on the horizon. The number three symbolically represents past, present and future, reminding us that past experiences provide valuable lessons for current situations, as well as those yet to come. The three ravens are echoed by the trinity of skulls that lie on the mist-shrouded ground, reminding us that others have traveled this path and met with a tragic fate. Representing an element of unknown danger, the skulls warn the traveler to tread cautiously when entering unfamiliar territory. Though he would be wise to take heed, these superstitious omens and warnings do not deter the Fool, who relentlessly proceeds forward.

The green moss and twisted branches of the barren tree indicate growth and development that can either flourish or constrict itself. Twin greenmen faces are sculpted into the archway stones on either side of the portal. Although their ominous expressions are ones of woe, they represent ancient wisdom that awaits within the unexplored territory that lies ahead. One need only know where to look and ask the right questions to gain the answers they seek.

ARTWORK TITLE: REALM OF SHADOWS (1998)

The artwork for the Fool was originally created as the CD cover for the album *Realm of Shadows,* one of Vargo's musical projects prior to forming Nox Arcana. The original painting portrayed only the solitary specter, without his wolf companion. The main figure was merely a faceless wraith, and a broken mask lay on the steps below. For the Tarot card, the wolf was added to the composition and the discarded mask upon the stairs was placed upon the specter's face to give it a human identity and also to add a harlequin persona to the figure.

"The masked phantom who lingers at the threshold to the realm of shadows was the ideal image to depict the Fool in the Gothic Tarot, representing the curious traveler, unaware of the forces that surround him," Vargo relates.

"Wolves and ravens are among my favorite earthly creatures to paint. Various ancient cultures believed that both of these creatures were messengers from the spirit realm. Edgar Allan Poe's classic poem 'The Raven' forever endeared these birds to a gothic audience and the Old World beliefs that witches and vampires could shapeshift into wolves likewise linked these predatory animals with a shadowy and supernatural connotation. Many people identify with both of these animals as their Ka, or spirit guardian. Combining them in this image allowed me to utilize aspects of mythology and folklore to convey the sense that, although he walks alone, mystical forces surround the traveler on his journey.

"I utilize the color green in my paintings to represent other-worldly power. Because it is an unnatural color for fog, the eerie green hue gives the subliminal impression that some unknown magic is at work. The archway in the crumbling stone wall remains intact because the keystone is still in place, representing a fragile yet solid structure that stands at the threshold between our dreams and that which is tangible."

I

THE MAGICIAN

I. THE MAGICIAN

A great harnessing of power, a link to the spirit world, a wealth of creativity and knowledge, a strong will, much self-confidence. Reversed: Weakness of the mind, a tendency to abuse power.

Divinatory meaning: The Magician commands a great knowledge of the arcane crafts and is highly skilled at utilizing the natural forces of the universe. Concentrate your efforts upon that which you want most in life, for it is within your power to make it happen. The elements are yours to command, granting you the necessary tools to complete your goals. Consider the surrounding resources that are at your disposal and recognize them for their true worth. Use your own ingenuity to manifest and attain that which you desire most. The Magician possesses a wealth of creativity and is able to focus his thoughts clearly. If this card is reversed, it signifies a misuse of power, laziness, and a neglect of natural resources.

Five cloaked figures perform a mystical ceremony upon the stone steps of a ritual altar. An enormous megalith, symbol of ancient mysticism, looms behind them. The alchemical sign of the oroboros is engulfed in the ritual fire above a pagan tabernacle made of three skulls. The Magician stands before the flaming oroboros with his left hand suspended above it. His right hand, which is raised to the heavens, summons a lightning bolt which strikes his palm.

The central figure reflects the traditional pose of the Magician in earlier decks, showing the sorcerer channeling the energy of the universe. The Magician is able to create what he truly desires from the elements that surround him, reminding us of the physical and spiritual resources at our disposal.

The mystical oroboros symbol replaces the sign of infinite power that customarily floats above the Magician's head and the lightning bolt is used to represent the universal energy that the

Magician harnesses and channels. The lightning is focused through the Magician, who acts as a conduit, directing and controlling the powers at his command.

Each of the other faceless ritual attendants holds one of the four suit icons. A wand, a cup, a sword and a pentacle are tightly clasped within their hands. Although traditional Tarot imagery depicts the Magician alone with his tools, here each of the four elements is offered by its own personal subject within the ritual, who lend their energy to the Magician to utilize as he sees fit. The conjured oroboros represents the elusive fifth element, or quintessence, that of timeless ether.

The Magician himself is cloaked in a green ritual robe, representing supernatural power in communion with the forces of nature. He harbors a vast knowledge of the mysteries of the universe as well as the tangible sciences and mathematics. The Magician possesses great will power and though he stands between fire and lightning, he remains steadfast and focused on his goal. The base of the staircase emerges from a sea of mist, showing that the Magician's actions are not bound by conventional ideas or limited to mundane practices.

The Magician has the vision to see the worth of everything that surrounds him and he has the knowledge to use these things to attain his heart's desire; however, his powers are beguiling and can easily be misused. For this reason, he can be either a helpful ally or a formidable adversary. In either case, he should be given great respect.

The ritual fire ring is supported by three skulls, once again representing past, present and future. However, unlike the haphazard pattern of skulls depicted in the Fool, these death's heads are neatly arranged in a uniform design, suggesting a structured plan.

The nighttime setting for the Magician's ceremony suggests that, unlike most mortals, he does not fear the darkness. In fact, the Magician derives much of his power from forces that are cloaked in shadow and hidden from the eyes of more timid men.

ARTWORK TITLE: SEVENTH SON (1994)

The original 1986 painting, entitled *Baptism in Fire,* was adapted three additional times to become the version used for the Gothic Tarot. The earliest version showed an infant floating in the ritual fire, unharmed by the surrounding flames. *Seventh Son,* the version prior to the Tarot card adaptation, refers to the ceremony in which a father and his six elder sons bestow mystical gifts to the newest child, born the seventh son of a seventh son. Such a child is said to be gifted in mysterious ways, often possessing foresight and other supernatural abilities.

A lover of mystical and hidden symbolism, Vargo utilized a secret alphabet for the staircase inscriptions to give perceptive viewers hidden insight into the true nature of the gifts that the original six attendants bore. These gifts included a scale, representing justice; a book, representing wisdom; a crown, representing power; a sword, representing strength; a chalice, representing healing; and a crystal ball, representing clairvoyance.

Vargo reveals, "The top step held the encrypted title *Seventh Son,* and although the lettering is quite small when reduced to Tarot card size, I felt the staircase inscriptions should be included, as each gift was appropriate to the Magician.

"The shadowy, hooded figures that stand before the formation of megaliths were inspired by the ancient Druids, who were believed to have built Stonehenge. According to legends, the druids were pagan magicians who held burning rituals to commune with the spirit realm. I can't explain why I was compelled to create four different versions of this image, each with subtle changes, but this scene kept playing out in my head. When it came time to begin putting the Gothic Tarot together, it was obvious to me that this painting should be used for the Magician card.

"The oroboros, depicted as a serpent devouring its own tail, is an ancient alchemical symbol for the infinite cycle of life. If you look very closely at some of the traditional Tarot images of the Magician, you can see that he wears a belt comprised of a snake biting its own tail."

II

THE HIGH PRIESTESS

II. THE HIGH PRIESTESS

Wise, calm and sure, possessing an intuitive nature, mysterious and secretive, also tenacious or deceptive at times, having scientific knowledge. Reversed: Passionate, conceited, defensive, a know-it-all.

Divinatory meaning: The High Priestess bestows us with a newfound psychic awareness that allows us to comprehend the mysteries of life. As the keeper of the divine word, the High Priestess knows many secrets, and thus holds the key to unlocking our true potential. Through peaceful meditation and honest inner reflection, we can channel her divine energy and gain an enhanced sense of intuition. The High Priestess is a learned woman and possesses an indomitable will. She is a reliable guide in spiritual matters and exhibits great composure, even under the most trying of circumstances. If this card is reversed, it symbolizes a self-important person who offers unnecessary advice.

An exotic Egyptian priestess stands in a temple archway, her hands resting upon black stone walls adorned with numerous hieroglyphic inscriptions. Her ceremonial headdress illustrates her position of power, and her posture suggests austere confidence. Her eyes glow with an otherworldly light, to imply that she can see beyond the scope of the mortal realm.

The High Priestess is adorned with the crown of the goddess Hathor, a traditional headpiece that symbolizes feminine powers. The *ankh*, a mystical symbol of life and fertility, decorates her breastplate, signifying that she is imbued with creative energy and a vibrant life-force. Another ankh is engraved above the temple entryway, signifying the mysterious powers of the universe that lie within. The left pillar holds the sculpted likeness of Khonsu, the Egyptian god of the moon, while the right pillar depicts the jackal-headed Anubis, guide of the Underworld. The ancient deities serve to remind us that the High Priestess resides within the arcane realm of shadows, where life's great mysteries lie hidden.

Unseen, she watches from the confines of her dark domain, waiting to emerge and bestow her gifts of occult knowledge to those who call upon her and summon her forth. She does not share her wisdom with those who do not actively seek it. In order to gain from her vast knowledge, we must respect her insight and adhere to her guidance. In this way, she shows us that spiritual strength and wisdom can be attained through divine reverence.

Despite her passive nature, the High Priestess conveys a sense of power, inner confidence and sensuality. Her voluptuous form, immodest wardrobe, and brazen sexuality suggest a seductive approach to a current situation, yet her seductive demeanor is deliberate and calculated, as opposed to wild and spontaneous. In this way she may use subtle and clever deception to mask her true intentions.

The High Priestess is also tenacious in her resolve. If you set your heart on a goal, you must dedicate yourself to attaining it. This may demand a change in your daily routine that may require physical labor, extensive study, or a strengthening of spirit. If you truly wish to achieve something, you may have to completely adjust your priorities, immerse yourself in your current project, and commit yourself to reaching your objective.

The High Priestess awakens the psychic powers within us and teaches us to follow our intuition. She is an avatar of the spiritual realm who allows us to commune with the mysterious plane beyond. By enabling us to clearly channel the divine powers of the universe, the High Priestess brings us hope and guides us in our darkest moments.

Besides her mystical abilities, the High Priestess is also well-versed in the known sciences, dating back to the alchemists of ancient Egypt. Such knowledge can be utilized with great results by those who choose to pursue this course of study and focus their minds upon it. In this way, the High Priestess can assist with both spiritual and physical matters.

ARTWORK TITLE: EGYPTIAN PRIESTESS (1996)

Created as part of an Egyptian triptych, this piece was an artistic homage to Anne Rice's literary vampire queen, Akasha. Vargo reveals a life-long fascination with ancient Egyptian art.

Vargo utilizes the predominant blue tones in many of his works as a visual technique to enhance the gothic appeal of the artwork, as well as to give his Tarot deck greater continuity. The color tones in some works were later changed to comply with this overall vision, as in the case of *Egyptian Priestess,* which was originally rendered in black and white.

"I depict many of my characters with glowing eyes as a subliminal way to portray them as supernatural beings with unearthly powers," Vargo explains. "The priestess' luminous eyes remind us of her ability to see deep into the spiritual realms, reinforcing her role as the keeper of divine knowledge.

"The unique style of Egyptian sculpture and architecture has always held a particular fascination for me, especially when compared to other works of the same era in nearby countries such as Greece and Rome.

"The frame of hieroglyphics that surrounds the High Priestess was included in all three works of my Egyptian triptych to lend a sense of architectural cohesiveness to the trio. While the framework is comprised of actual hieroglyphs from the ancient Egyptian language, the design was arranged strictly as an artistic element. In each of the three pieces, the gods Anubis and Khonsu adorn the supporting columns of the chamber. These were chosen to depict different realms of darkness, specifically the mysterious blackness of the Underworld and the illuminated night sky. In this case the column figures suggest that the High Priestess holds dominion over the shadows."

III

THE EMPRESS

III. The Empress

A giver of life, nurturing, a dominant and active female, self-indulgent at times, signifying passion, sexuality and fertility. Reversed: Truth, diplomacy, difficulty expressing emotion, indecisive.

Divinatory meaning: The Empress signifies a strong female persona and represents the most prevalent feminine influence in your life at the current time. As a mother figure, she is a symbol of fertility, which can either be a literal interpretation or symbolically refer to one's productivity. She is also a nurturing presence, who feeds and reinforces your self-esteem. The Empress helps to attain the things you are most passionate about, be it in areas of romance or career goals. Your creative energies are at their peak. Now is the time to focus your efforts inward and put yourself above the interest of others. If this card is reversed, it signifies a callous demeanor and brutal honesty, as well as a person who avoids taking sides in a debate.

A vampire queen, draped in a silken gown, emerges from a coffin in an ornate tomb flanked by sculpted angels of death. Her mouth is slightly opened, allowing us a glimpse of her predatory fangs.

Vargo references the ancient Hebrew legend of Lilith for his own Empress, identifying her as the queen of all vampires. In medieval lore, Lilith was created by God to be the first wife of Adam. Having been cast out of the Garden of Eden for refusing to serve Adam, she became a legendary figure as the mother of all demons and creatures of darkness. Lilith's infamous legends of procreation convey the concept of motherhood that is associated with the Empress.

The demeanor of the Gothic Empress is greatly different than the traditional depiction, which portrays her as a matronly queen who resides upon her throne with peaceful dignity. In contrast, Vargo's Empress is passionate and seductive. She is an enticingly beautiful creature of the night who has been awakened from her eternal slumber. As she rises from her resting place, her hands clutch the sides of the casket with great tension, and her face conveys a look of contempt. Her left foot emerges from her coffin and her clawed toes suggest that she is no mere mortal. The jeweled crown upon her head denotes that she is of royal blood and a presence that commands authority while the skeletal angels beside her coffin remind the viewer that this creature is most comfortable within her natural domain.

The ferocious and passionate animation of the Empress emphasizes the undying vigor that is required to obtain our hearts' desires. Just as the Empress exudes a vibrant energy, we must possess a similar inner fire in order to successfully attain what we seek in life. Pursuing that which you are most passionate about will enable you to accomplish your goal with greater ease. Indulge your whims to clear and focus your mind. Establishing a comfortable work environment, whether at home or in the workplace, will greatly enhance your creative process.

Just as the Emperor is seen as the dominant male principle of the Tarot, the Empress embodies the ruling female force. Together, they can manifest great things. The unification of the masculine and feminine energies results in creation. Whereas the Emperor molds the form, the Empress possesses the ability to nurture it and breathe life into it.

The Empress is also a symbol of natural sexual expression. She represents the mysterious and irresistible feminine allure. She does not intentionally seduce her mate by flaunting her feminine wiles, but instead allows him to follow the inevitable course of nature.

The Empress may seem overly protective at times, but she has only the best of intentions for her children and loyal subjects, and thus her maternal instincts are to be closely heeded. Nurture your ideas and allow them to grow and they will soon take on a life of their own.

ARTWORK TITLE: LILITH (1996)

As the final part of Vargo's gothic triptych depicting the three faces of the vampire, *Lilith* expresses the sensual and enticing aspects of this dark creature of the night. The title "Lilith" was also used in *Tales from the Dark Tower* to mark the Dark Queen's tomb within the Tower's catacombs. Sealed within this forsaken burial vault, the Queen of Shadows seeks her escape from this veritable prison to reign upon the mortal world once more.

"The Lilith myth is an intriguing tale with an uncertain moral that is open for interpretation," Vargo explains. "Lilith defies God and is cast from Eden, and though she survives to rule her own dynasty, her children are considered to be abominations. Whether you perceive her as being the heroine or the villain of the tale, there's no denying that she is a strong-willed female who answers to no man. This made her the ideal choice as the symbolic representation of the Gothic Empress.

"Since the Empress is designated as the number three card in the Major Arcana, the numerological symbolism also came into play in this design. Aside from the triple archway above her head, the Empress also reflects the number three with her three-pointed crown and the triple armbands and bracelets that adorn her. In addition, her figure forms a trinity with the two winged skeletons that stand guard at the entrance to her domain.

"To give this image an authentic gothic feel, I chose to render it in pencil, creating a stark contrast between the deathly white flesh of the vampire and the pitch-black shadows that surround her. The stonework and architecture of Gothic burial vaults and crypts is an art form unto itself and the setting for this piece reflects the ornate Old-World craftsmanship and masonry that was used to decorate the tombs of kings and queens."

IV

THE EMPEROR

IV. THE EMPEROR

A figure of authority, stability and protection, a reasonable and responsible character, good self-control, firm yet fair. Reversed: Compassionate and benevolent, domineering and a tendency to be inflexible.

Divinatory meaning: Representing ultimate authority, control and prestige, the domineering Emperor is in total command of his surroundings. He signifies a confident leader who possesses great spiritual and physical strength. Take charge of the matter facing you and use diplomacy to attain a firm resolve. Use your knowledge and experience to determine what is best for those around you. Be poised and don't make any rash decisions without first weighing all the pertinent elements. Be fair and contemplate all factors before taking action, but stand strong in your final decision. If this card is reversed, it signifies someone who is overly emotional, tyrannical and uncompromising.

Seated on a Gothic throne covered in red velvet, the vampire lord Dracula is surrounded by his three undead brides. His right hand rests upon a black wolf at his side, while a raven is ominously perched on top of the throne.

Representing a strong and domineering male influence, the Emperor is the governing ruler of the Tarot. He denotes a strong-willed father figure who is controlling and protective. Representing tradition, leadership and authority, the Emperor signifies one's dynasty. Like the traditional father figure, the Emperor must consider the effect that his actions will have on those closest to him, as well as his ongoing legacy. His three beautiful brides, though they are his consorts and companions, are also his undead offspring, given immortal life through his vampiric powers. His successors act as an eternal testament to his deeds that allows his legacy to flourish.

The Emperor's esteem and position of command is artistically established by Dracula's seat in this place of honor. The Emperor is surrounded by his family and minions, illustrating how everything in his realm revolves around him. The jeweled ring that the Emperor wears on his left hand further denotes the stable concepts of marriage and family.

Three gothic animal totems surround the Emperor, each symbolizing an aspect of the vampire lord's mysterious and foreboding character. The raven symbolizes a grim harbinger of unknown and dark tidings, while the wolf represents a loyal subject who can act on his master's behalf, presenting a fierce and deadly adversary to the Emperor's foes. Vampires have traditionally been associated with their namesake bats, due to their nocturnal nature and the fact that they both gain nourishment from the blood of their victims. The vibrant red coloration of Dracula's throne and cape are a symbolic reference to blood, which embodies the life force of all vampires. Spectral faces appear in the mist as a subtle reminder that the vampire lord governs not only men and beasts, but the realm of the undead as well.

Two skulls can be seen on the steps, warning of the dangers of opposing the Emperor's decree. These macabre mementos also serve as grim reminders of past encounters with those who would dare invade the sanctity of Dracula's domain. This idea is further conveyed through the depiction of the closest bride, who rests her clawed hand upon her macabre trophy with sinister delight.

The Emperor represents both a man of action and an analytical thinker who can weigh all factors, arrive at a fair decision and enforce his will without hesitation or question. His decree may sometimes be uncompromising and his actions ruthless, but his verdicts are in the best interest of those he governs. He is often a philosophical person, and though he may have many advisors, the decisions he reaches are ultimately his own. The Emperor is protective, forceful and wise, and thus his laws should be heeded without question.

ARTWORK TITLE: DRACULA (1998)

Vargo's portrait of the vampire lord was painted to commemorate the 100th anniversary of the publication of Bram Stoker's novel, *Dracula*. Just as Stoker blended history and imagination to create one legendary character, Vargo sought to artistically blend portraits of the historical Romanian prince Vlad Dracul III and imagery from Stoker's classic work of fiction into this singular painting.

"Dracula, both the literary and historical figure, represents the ultimate gothic image of immortal authority and control," Vargo relates.

"The legacy of Vlad Dracul, otherwise known as Dracula, was one of ruthless and uncompromising leadership. After being imprisoned by the Turkish Sultan in the 15th century, Vlad was released and returned to Romania where he began his quest to rid his beloved homeland of Turkish occupation. Vlad claimed the Romanian throne and began a bloody reign of executing criminals, corrupt noblemen and clergymen alike. His favorite method of execution was to impale his enemies alive on tall wooden stakes, leaving their bodies on public display as grisly reminders of the terrible fate that awaited those who opposed him.

"His ruthless measures were quite effective during those primitive times and kept invading armies at bay during his reign. To this day, Dracula is heralded as a national hero in Romania; however, according to legend, his savage acts and consequent excommunication from the Church have doomed his spirit to wander the earth as one of the undead. Due to Bram Stoker's fictional embellishments of this historical monarch, Dracula's legacy remains immortal, as all emperors would intend.

"In European folklore, the vampire is also believed to be a shape-shifter. Dracula's animal minions and the ghostly mist that surrounds them also represent the various forms and guises he can transform into. I wanted to incorporate the popular elements from history, fiction and lore and blend them together to create the ultimate portrait of Dracula."

V

THE HIGH PRIEST

V. THE HIGH PRIEST

Spiritual wisdom, faithfulness and mercy, strictly traditional values, a reluctance to explore new paths. Reversed: Socially skilled, a firm grasp of reality, a weakness for indulging the needs of others.

Divinatory meaning: Rigid in Old-World values, the High Priest advances our understanding of our inner self when we are faced with social or moral pressures. Tradition and honor bind him to serving a higher cause that leads to enlightenment. Spiritual communion through prayer, meditation or ritual grants us communion with the Divine, allowing us to partake of sublime wisdom. The High Priest manifests himself as a loyal friend or sympathetic confidant who advises to have faith and not to stray from the righteous path. If this card is reversed, it represents one who relies on logic over faith as well as someone who suffers as a result of putting the needs of others before his own.

An ancient vampire cloaked in black rests in the confines of his coffin. The menacing creature assumes a deathly repose with his arms crossed over his chest as he peers outward with glowing eyes. The chiseled images of two skeletal angels adorn the columns beside the undead creature, mimicking his pose. His faithful stone servants remind us that this vampire's sacred will demands our unquestioning compliance.

The High Priest is a wise and pious elder whose powers of insight make him a trusted confidant and respected advisor. He is the masculine figure of all dark wisdom and arcane knowledge. The traditional Tarot associations of higher learning and established traditions are artistically suggested by Vargo in this vampire's physical look. His gaunt appearance and skull-like visage convey his great age, suggesting an ancient wisdom. His glowing eyes illustrate his unearthly vision to see both the material and spiritual realms, and thus he should be respected for his supernatural ability to accurately assess the situation before him.

The High Priest is a revered relic of the ancient world, and thus serves as a reminder of the old ways. This strict adherence to familiar territory may feel safe, but it restricts us from trying new things and ideas that typically lead to physical progress and growth. Yet the wisdom of the High Priest is essential for the growth of the mind and spirit.

The High Priest rejects the modern ways, insisting that his own ways are proven and have withstood the test of time. He does not conform to radical new ways of thinking, and his Old-World mindset offers the true wisdom of the ages. Possessing an incredible ability to see directly to the heart of the matter and shrewdly detect the true nature of a situation or person, the High Priest is often starkly accurate in his assessments and domineering in his approach to problem solving. He stands firm in his inner convictions due to his unshakable personal faith.

A personification of organized religion as well as occult and mystical knowledge, the High Priest is an exalted soul who is highly perceptive with regard to spiritual matters. To find solace in the knowledge he shares is to know true contentment, while ignoring his wisdom may lead to a stifling of the inner self.

Seen here in a position of rest, his tranquility suggests deep spiritual meditation and inner reflection. The two skeletal angels that flank his sides symbolize his power in the realm of the dead as well as the living. The two supplicants, who are traditionally depicted as kneeling before the High Priest, are represented here by the skeletal figures who share the same reverent pose.

The crossed keys, which were traditionally depicted below the feet of the High Priest to symbolize the way to unlock the secret knowledge of the conscious and subconscious, are symbolically represented here by the crossed arms of the three figures.

Above all, the High Priest is a vessel of the higher powers of the universe who acts on their behalf, granting communion with the Divine. Seek guidance from one who possesses a greater wisdom and heed their insights to unlock the mysteries of the spiritual realm.

ARTWORK TITLE: NOSFERATU (1996)

As the second of Vargo's vampire triptych, this work was created to express the more horrific aspects of the legendary creature. *Nosferatu* is an old European term for "the undead." Such supernatural legends abound in early European folklore and the physical look of Vargo's ghoulish creature pays tribute to F.W. Murnau's classic silent film, *Nosferatu*. Vargo chose the moniker High Priest over the title of Hierophant to reinforce this figure's position of austere command and exalted prestige.

Vargo shares his creative insights. "The vampire seen here is an ancient creature whose wisdom has kept him alive through countless ages until his humanity has all but disappeared. His cadaverous appearance conveys the idea that even though his physical body has deteriorated, his spirit is immortal. The knowledge he has accumulated spans the centuries and encompasses all realms of learning, with an emphasis on the occult and the spiritual mysteries of life.

"Resting within the confines of his coffin, the Gothic High Priest is comfortable within the boundaries of his domain. At times he enters a meditative dormant state, during which he ponders the true purpose of his existence. As a man of faith, he believes in the grand universal scheme and the idea that all men have a destined role to play.

"In contrast to the seductive vampires that abound in many of my other paintings, I chose to portray this vampire as a ghoulish undead creature in order to convey the ideas of the loathsome vampiric demons depicted in ancient folklore. Many of these tales tell of revenant souls who clawed their way out of the grave to prey upon the living, sending their souls to the Devil. These hideous, walking corpses were often described as having rotting flesh, clawed fingers and razor-sharp teeth that filled their mouths."

VI

THE LOVERS

VI. THE LOVERS

Sexual attraction, beauty and love, a moral choice to be made, the drawing together of opposites, difficulties overcome. Reversed: Problematic relationship, opposition, rebellion against authority.

Divinatory meaning: The Lovers signify that romance and sexual desires abound and that a physical union or a uniting of two ideas will lead to success. Let passion be your guide, but use discretion and be mindful of your affairs. Opposites attract one another to form a unified bond. Abide by the moral decisions you make and accept responsibility for all consequences of your actions. Past obstacles can now be overcome by acting together with the right partner. Your true love is within your grasp, but a sacrifice may be required before you can find happiness together. Follow your heart and surrender yourself to the power of love. If this card is reversed, it signifies two opposing forces that repel each other or a love affair that is one-sided.

A suave male vampire embraces his beautiful female victim and leans close to drink from her delicate throat. As she willingly offers her neck to him, her open mouth and closed eyes portray a moment of rapture. Her immortal lover clutches her intently, savoring her life's blood as he brings her across the threshold of darkness. Twin skeletal angels stand guard at the domain of the undead, marking the gateway of the dark realm of paradise that the Lovers will soon inhabit together.

Older Tarot renditions depict the Lovers card as a man with two women at his side, representing a matter of emotional choices. In Vargo's rendition, the connotation of choice is suggested by the victim's decision to succumb to the vampire who embraces her, thus surrendering her mortality to him. It is also implied by his choice to end her mortal existence and sustain her once more by bringing her across the threshold of darkness.

In tales of ancient lore, before the maiden and the prince can live happily ever after, they must first prove their devotion through a sacrifice. This concept is illustrated in Vargo's vision of the Lovers card as the female sacrifices her mortal soul to be with her immortal love. Devotion, commitment and sacrifice are among our heart's most noble and selfless pursuits. Such choices in life are the result of decisions made by following our deepest passions. The Lovers dictate that emotion should be held in high esteem above heartless logic and calculated reason.

The emotional connotations of Vargo's artwork are intensely evocative. In capturing this moment of dark rapture, the portrait illustrates the union of opposites such as male and female, innocence and lust, as well as mortal death and immortal life. Although the concept of combining such opposing principles might seem destined to produce catastrophic results, the consummation of the Lovers' forbidden act brings unknown levels of sensual bliss. In this way the Lovers represent an ideal of perfect harmony, created by the blending of various diverse elements that complement one another.

The Lovers symbolize the unification of ideas to form one cohesive plan. This blissful partnership teaches that more can be achieved by working together with a partner than by both individuals working alone. This reinforces the spiritual concept of soul mates, wherein two separate individuals feel drawn together by destiny to become one complete soul.

If your love has been unrequited in the past, now is the time to renew your efforts. Your sexual prowess is at its peak. Use this opportunity to explore newfound realms of sensuality and romance. Follow your heart, succumb to your deepest desires and only pursue the things you are most passionate about.

The Lovers, while a familiar symbol of romantic pursuits, also remind us to use discretion in our affairs. Your present situation may require a moral choice or commitment. A sordid affair might satisfy temporary lusts but may ultimately have devastating results. Be prepared to honor any vows you make and to abide by your ethical decisions.

ARTWORK TITLE: VAMPIRE'S KISS (1996)

In Vargo's original version of this rendering, the Latin phrase *Noctem Aerternus,* meaning "eternal night," is etched in the stone above the Lovers' arch, marking the threshold of the realm of darkness. The inscription was cropped for the Tarot image, as were the inscriptions above the Empress and High Priest images, to eliminate any conflict with the card titles.

"This image was the first part of my vampire triptych, portraying the three faces of this undead creature," Vargo explains. "There's a certain primal appeal about it, as it illustrates the romantic seduction to the darkside. In the *Dark Tower* mythos, this rendering was used to illustrate the story 'Vampire's Kiss,' in which the vampire lord Brom brings his beloved Rianna across the threshold of darkness. Rianna willingly offers herself to him, sacrificing her mortal life and soul to be with her true love. Brom's unrestrained moment of passion inevitably leads him to unforeseen heartache thereafter.

"Even though this piece is just a small pencil rendering, *Vampire's Kiss* is one of my most popular works of art. It really struck a chord with my gothic audience, and I've received a lot of positive comments on it throughout the years. There's a deep, sensual eroticism associated with vampires.

"The vampire, though considered a monster by most, is also seen as the ultimate seducer, representing mystery, danger and forbidden passion. Over the centuries, vampires have evolved from the sinister abominations of ancient lore to become romanticized as the seductive and irresistible anti-hero of modern fiction and film. My artistic intent with this illustration was to capture all of these alluring aspects.

"To enhance the black and white artwork, one small trickle of red was added running along the woman's throat when the image was reproduced as a journal cover. For the Gothic Tarot, an additional shade of blue was applied to the rendering in order to fit the color scheme of the deck."

VII

THE CHARIOT

VII. THE CHARIOT

Triumph in battle, a forceful character, the need of firm emotional control, one who is vengeful. Reversed: Quarrel, upheaval, a weakness of will, a dispute which may result in litigation and defeat.

Divinatory meaning: The Chariot teaches us to take the reins and steer your life in the direction you truly wish to pursue. By just going along for the ride, you may never be able to reach your desired goal. Concentrate your efforts to persuade the forces at your command to help you attain that which you truly desire. Accept the fact that some things may be beyond your grasp at this time, then set your sights on that which you can attain. Concentrate your efforts to get past adversity and momentous changes. Avoid passivity and accept responsibility for your life by focusing your will power and taking decisive action. If this card is reversed, it signifies an indecisive nature or a conflict of interests that cannot be resolved.

Two ebony steeds with demonic red eyes pull a black coach through the dead of night. A mysterious figure in a top hat and cape drives the carriage with determined resolve. A dense fog engulfs the path ahead as skeletal tree branches reach out from the surrounding darkness.

As the horses swiftly draw the carriage through the mist-shrouded terrain, one can clearly see that without a driver, all hope of arriving safely at the intended destination is lost. The Chariot symbolizes moments in our lives when destiny offers us numerous paths to pursue. At these crossroads we can either choose to take the reins and steer, or allow our lives to be guided by someone else. You must decide whether you want to be a leader who works diligently to keep your team moving in the right direction toward the desired goal, or be a complacent follower who may not do any of the difficult work, but as a result may never reach your intended destination.

This concept is further illustrated by Vargo's depiction of the coach itself, which portrays it as a hearse that is presumably ferrying a lifeless person to the grave. The Chariot shows us that we can choose to take control of our own destiny and truly live, or we can merely exist as life passes us by.

Two contrasting forces, traditionally symbolized by a black and white sphinx, are represented here as the choices of control and submission, free will and helplessness. The Chariot allows us to realize that life presents us with many decisions and we can either take an active or passive approach to achieving our goals.

In reference to Gothic literature, this card suggests Jonathan Harker's carriage ride in *Dracula,* as he is brought through the Carpathian Mountains to the Count's castle by a mysterious driver. Harker, who is whisked along treacherous roads, is swept into a series of uncontrollable events that alter the course of his life in dramatic ways.

While the driver takes charge of the horses by keeping a firm grip on the reins, he must be wary of forces that are beyond his ability to command, illustrated here by the dense fog. Even as we hold the reins, we are just as likely to lose control of the beasts, as they may be unwilling to yield to their master's will.

The Chariot also symbolizes momentous changes that may affect our lives. These events can be controlled by our will power and sheer determination. While braving new territory, be aware of your surroundings to accommodate sudden changes. Maintain a constant focus on the path ahead and be prepared to adjust for any detours or unforeseen obstacles that may arise.

The Chariot may also signify a physical journey that spans a great distance and leads to new opportunities. This card also symbolizes emotional control that lets us conquer our anxieties and fears. The Chariot can have either a positive or negative effect in our lives depending upon how we react to the new opportunities and responsibilities that present themselves along our journey.

Artwork Title: "The Black Coach (2002)

Created specifically for the deck, Vargo describes his moment of inspiration for this painting as a vivid dream he had in which a ghostly black coach drawn by two shadowy steeds mysteriously soared through the sky, landing in the street outside his childhood home. However, Vargo relates, the carriage in the painting differs greatly from the spectral version in his vision.

"For the Chariot in the Gothic Tarot, I briefly considered utilizing traditional Egyptian elements, such as the opposing Sphinxes which are customarily depicted pulling the coach. However, I quickly decided that, while I enjoy depicting Egyptian motifs, a hearse would make for a much more appropriate Chariot in a deck of Gothic Tarot cards. When I was much younger, I had this very vivid dream about a ghostly old-fashioned carriage, so I decided that I should utilize my vision for this card.

"The coach itself is rendered from a three-quarter perspective, making it difficult to discern if it is actually a passenger carriage or a hearse. This intentional ambiguity allows the viewer to determine the severity of the Chariot's message.

"Instead of the Chariot being pulled in two possible directions, the choice here is one of being either the driver or the passenger. One can either take charge of the reins and steer his followers along the righteous path or one can merely sit back and enjoy the ride, while exerting no control, input or guidance as to the final destination.

"The idea that you can make a difference and steer the course of your own destiny is a concept that I strongly believe in. Unfortunately, most people are quite content to sit in the comfort of the Chariot and enjoy the scenery while a determined few actually commit to achieving the goals they set. One of the key factors to success is to take the driver's seat and not become complacent."

VIII

JUSTICE

VIII. Justice

An impartial and honest point of view, to reach and abide by a fair decision, reaping what one sows, putting right past wrongs. Reversed: Bigotry, a biased decision, severe in administering punishment.

Divinatory meaning: The deeds of the past shall be answered for, and the repercussions will be swift and just. Your actions will result in deserved consequences. Now is the time of atonement for past indiscretions, as well as a time to reap the accolades for good deeds and rewards for hard work. A fair and balanced outlook is needed to see things clearly and to help you attain your current goals. Allow your moral convictions to guide your actions. Fate has leveled the playing field. Those who have been wronged will be avenged and the guilty will suffer. In legal matters, this card foretells that justice will prevail and the scales will be set right once more. If this card is reversed, it signifies an unfair decision, a biased personal outlook, unwarranted praise or an undeservedly harsh punishment.

A crimson-clad angel soars through the night sky on black wings. Her sword held before her in a defiant pose, she is the defender of truth and a vanquisher of injustice and evil. Her face is uplifted toward her gilded weapon and the darkened heavens above.

Depicted as a female warrior, Justice is the avatar of truth who exposes past wrongs and sets them right. Unlike the traditional personification of Justice, she is not blind or passive, but a relentless avenging angel that takes action as judge, jury and, if need be, executioner. She has the authority and power to punish and reward those deserving.

The strength of this archetypal figure is emphasized by her sleek and muscular form as well as her battle-ready pose. Her noble mission is never-ending and she eternally rises to the challenge. Her power and conviction are signified by her stern and unrelenting posture, as well as the formidable weapon she wields, identifying her as an avenging crusader.

Both sides of her golden scale rest equally balanced, and her grip upon it is firm, indicating that it requires some measure of effort to assure that a fair judgement will be reached. Yet the angel effortlessly wields her sword high overhead, and her body is lithe with power and readiness, indicating that once a decision is made, any action required will be quickly dealt. The emphasis on the horizontal blade reinforces the level of the scale, further emphasizing the concept of balance and equilibrium.

Universal justice, otherwise known as Karma, is a force beyond our human ability to control. It is the belief that our actions, whether good or bad, will be revisited upon us by fate. We can only strive to shape a positive destiny by following the path of righteousness. Just as our previous actions shape our present conditions, our present actions will also shape our future. You may rely on the concept of universal Justice, trusting that truth and righteousness will prevail in a current situation, or you may choose to become directly involved in seeing that justice is served.

The Justice card represents the laws of the universe in the forms of spiritual rewards and retribution, as well as the laws of the material world. In regard to legal disputes such as a court case or other litigation, this card signifies that justice will indeed prevail in the matter at hand.

Justice is also a symbol of equality, and thus reminds us that we should enter into new endeavors and relationships without prejudice. If the odds seem to be stacked against you in a current situation, Justice will intervene to balance the scales.

Before embarking on a new venture, weigh the pros and cons against one another. It is important to remember that Justice holds us accountable for each and every decision we make. Compassionate thoughts and actions will be rewarded, while selfish deeds will warrant just retribution. What is sown will eventually be reaped.

ARTWORK TITLE: JUSTICE (1998)

Vargo mindfully sought to enhance the Gothic Tarot's Old World appeal by following the original Tarot traditions with the numbering of the Major Arcana. For his Tarot deck, Vargo chose to replace Justice as number eight in the Major Arcana, breaking from the Golden Dawn concept which switched the positions of Justice and Strength.

Vargo explains, "In the dawn of the 20th century, occult philosopher Alfred Edward Waite switched the numerical positions of the Justice and Strength cards in an attempt to make the Tarot coincide with the Kabbalah. A member of the Hermetic Order of the Golden Dawn, Waite was convinced that the Tarot was derived from ancient, mystical Hebrew texts and he took it upon himself to make changes in the Tarot traditions in order to make the Major Arcana conform to his concept.

"While I respect Waite for his idea of designing a fully illustrated Minor Arcana, I didn't see the merit in changing the traditional numbers of the Major Arcana. Many modern Tarot decks follow Waite's concept, copying his numerical changes without knowing the rationale behind his decision.

"For the Justice card, several artistic and symbolic changes were made to the existing painting in order to make it fit the aesthetics of the Gothic Tarot. The coloration of the original painting was changed from vibrant yellow and gold to deep tones of scarlet and black. The painting also depicted the angel tightly clutching a round shield in her left hand. The angel's golden-white feathers were changed to raven black, and her shield was replaced with a balanced scale. A glowing aura of radiant red light was added as an artistic element to make her stand out against the stark black background, and also to give the impression that she is imbued with supernatural powers."

IX

THE HERMIT

IX. The Hermit

A period of contemplation, a search for wisdom, isolation and withdrawal from the world, a prudent nature, possible indicator of corruptive forces. Reversed: Paranoia, reclusive to the point of fearfulness.

Divinatory meaning: The Hermit represents one who has retreated from society to live in self-imposed exile in an effort to gain focus. Allow yourself to withdraw from others in order to achieve mental and spiritual clarity. Detach yourself from your current surroundings in order to collect and focus your thoughts and regain your own true understanding of a current situation. The peaceful confines of solitude will allow you to meditate, study and practice your craft without distraction. Take time away to contemplate a current dilemma. A new perspective will permit you to clearly see the obstacles in your path, allowing you to plot a clear course to your desired goal. If this card is reversed, it signifies extreme shyness as well as an unwarranted fear of confrontation.

A lone vampire regards the viewer with a solemn stare as he commands a swarm of bats to take flight from their belfry domain. A massive bell dominates the background, and fearsome winged gargoyles adorn the perch below. Isolated in his belfry tower, far removed from the world beneath him, the Hermit signifies withdrawal from social surroundings; however, his exile is a purposeful seclusion meant to bring about a deep sense of personal and spiritual enlightenment.

In times of duress, the psyche can often require complete solitude for meditation and inner reflection. By disconnecting from crowded environments, we can focus our attention to our most dire pursuits without diversion, and thus reach a clearer understanding of precise actions to take.

To gain a better perspective of matters, we often climb the highest summit, and in doing so, we are able to see the full landscape clearly. The Hermit isolates himself in a place where he can gain a new perspective as well—a vantage point secluded from the rest of the world. In doing so, he gains a new point of view, as well as the clarity he needs to better hear the voice within himself.

Shunning society often results in a loss of social skills and graces. The introverted Hermit cares little about current events and does not concern himself with worldly matters or proper etiquette. He is a recluse, and his self-imposed isolation keeps him far removed from the distractions of others. Without distractions he can maintain a clear mindset, allowing him to focus his time and efforts on his solo studies and intellectual pursuits.

In reference to older Tarot decks in which the Hermit carries an hourglass, the timepiece is reflected here by the tower bell, which strikes the hour to mark the passage of time. For thousands of years, bells have been used in Eastern religious ceremonies as a means to awaken our minds to the spiritual realm and invoke the powers of the Divine. In the West, vesper bells can serve a similar purpose for parishioners, summoning the faithful to hear the words of the Almighty.

Unlike traditional depictions, the Gothic Hermit does not carry a lantern to light the way in the darkness. Instead, he is a nocturnal creature who is more at home in the shadows than in the spotlight. His winged minions act as his eyes, enabling him to see great distances beyond the scope of his own nocturnal vision.

The Hermit can seem distant and contemplative, even when surrounded by people, and he constantly yearns for seclusion. Out of touch with society or modern ways, the Hermit is a sheltered soul and a loner who avoids confrontation and retreats into the shadows of a private comfort-zone where he is most at ease. Sequestered away, the Hermit can hone his craft without the influence of others, allowing him to heed the whispers of his own inner voice and fully explore the boundaries of his own creativity.

ARTWORK TITLE: BELFRY HAUNT (2000)

This illustration was used in the *Tales from the Dark Tower* anthology to illustrate the story, "Vesper Tolls," where the mysterious vampire lord known as the Baron has withdrawn from the world to keep eternal vigil over the nefarious legacy within the Dark Tower.

"The Baron locks himself away while studying the ancient scrolls and books in his library sanctum, desperately searching for a way to end his own plight," Vargo explains. "The Baron's self-imposed exile keeps him distant from humanity, for his sake and theirs. He will defend his domain to the death, if need be, in order to preserve his solitude.

"The sheer isolation of the Hermit's domain is suggested by his lofty belfry perch and the antiquated architecture of the tower itself. His right hand is raised against the wind in a gesture to command his winged emissaries to take to the night sky. As the tattered fringes of his ancient cloak billow behind him, we are reminded that he and his minions oppose the forces of nature, suggesting a mindset of going against that which is deemed normal.

"Unlike traditional Tarot depictions, the Gothic Hermit holds no walking stick, but instead rests his clawed hand upon the supporting ledge to steady himself. Below him, two ghoulish winged gargoyles act as his only companions, much like the stone grotesques befriended by Quasimodo, the monstrous bell ringer in *The Hunchback of Notre Dame*, who also withdraws from the world to hide within the confines of his sanctuary.

"Most introverts are misunderstood and not readily accepted into popular social circles. Although they are generally thoughtful, intelligent and philosophical, their shy and reserved nature seldom allows them to share their views with others. Many artists and writers shut themselves away from society as a means to create a more productive work environment. This allows them a private sanctuary in which to structure their creative ideas."

X

WHEEL OF FORTUNE

X. The Wheel of Fortune

The ever-evolving cycle of life, expect dramatic changes, destiny takes over, fortune and luck are prevalent forces. Reversed: Facing a challenge, controlling events, an over-abundance or increase.

Divinatory meaning: The Wheel of Fortune reminds us that life is a constant series of ups and downs. By being patient we can weather any storm, but we must also remember to cherish the good times while they last. The ongoing cycle of universal balance and change dictates that as one thing comes to an end, a new one is born. What you perceive as serendipity is actually part of a universal plan. A dynamic change in your life may cause you to experience a reversal of fortune. Luck is a principal force in your affairs at this time. Trust in destiny and put your faith in the hands of fate. If this card is reversed, it can signify too much of a good thing, confronting a dilemma, a long streak of bad luck or misfortune.

Two golden dragons follow one another around a circular motif beneath the gaze of four spiritual overseers. As one dragon rises, the other falls, symbolizing the concept of universal balance and perpetual change. The dragons' heads are turned to look back instead of forward, suggesting that they are more concerned with what lies behind them than they are of what lies ahead.

As the Wheel of Fortune turns, we encounter an ongoing series of high and low points in our lives. The perpetual cycle of creation and destruction, birth and death, are illustrated here by the twin dragon totems, which are reminiscent of the Chinese Yin-Yang design.

Just as daylight fades to darkest night, the dawning of a new day will surely follow. Keeping this in mind, the wheel teaches us to be patient during the bad times and to make the most of the good. The key to unlocking the mysteries in life is to understand that we must fully appreciate the current moment, without dwelling in the past or worrying about the future.

Whereas the Magician teaches us to forge our own destiny and the Chariot advises us to take control of our lives, the Wheel of Fortune tells us to trust in fate. Have faith in the great cosmic plan and allow destiny to govern the things that are beyond your physical control.

The Wheel of Fortune also foretells of periods of success that follow a duration of difficulty, as well as opportunities that arise at the most appropriate time, enabling us to act upon them immediately. The Wheel suggests that what has been planted is now being reaped and the bountiful fruits of our labors can now be harvested.

The golden tones of this design imply opulence and good fortune and the twin dragon motifs represent power, prosperity, good luck, protection, courage and wisdom. At the circle's center are four interlocking rings, suggesting the four suits of the Tarot, as well as the four elements of earth, air, fire and water. Each ring represents a piece of the grand universal design. Mystics teach that all life is interconnected and bound together, and that our actions affect everything around us, influencing and shaping the world in subtle ways.

Four gothic greenman faces replace the traditional depictions of the four Archangels residing in the corners. These kingly faces suggest ancient wisdom and signify the four winds, as well as the four seasons. These cosmic guardians surround the wheel to watch over us from the outer realms, ensuring universal balance between the offsetting forces.

Although the Wheel generally represents a reversal of luck or fortune, the appearance of this card typically suggests prosperity. In financial matters, it foretells of a windfall and great wealth, but it also warns against the pitfalls of becoming arrogant due to an overabundance of good fortune, reminding us that this too shall pass. Conversely, the Wheel promises that bad luck will not linger forever. When your spirit is crushed beneath the mounting weight of malignant forces, remember that the pressure being exerted is not limitless, and the Wheel of Fortune will ultimately bring relief.

Artwork Title: Wheel of Fortune (2002)

Created specifically for the Tarot, this elaborate design is another fine example of Vargo's powerful use of gothic symbolism. Historically, the Wheel of Fortune is an image that has appeared in tales concerning the quest for the Holy Grail, such as the Arthurian romances of the Middle Ages. In the 13th century French prose work, *La Mort le Roi Artu,* King Arthur has a dream in which a beautiful woman places him upon a wheel that is outfitted with many seats. Arthur's seat happens to be at the wheel's highest point and from this perspective he can gaze majestically out upon the world. However, the mysterious woman ominously informs him that he sits upon the Wheel of Fortune, and its cyclic movement will inevitably topple his kingdom.

"The Wheel of Fortune is a symbolic representation of the unending cycle of cosmic balance and flux," Vargo relates. "Because the Wheel is a universal principle that cannot be personified by a central character, I was presented with an artistic challenge. After much deliberation, I chose to transform the Wheel into an emblematic design to depict it as an icon of fate, much like the Chinese Tai Chi, otherwise known as the Yin-Yang symbol.

"I utilized dragons for the animal totems that traditionally circumvent the Wheel because of the mystical symbolism and various benevolent properties associated with them. Though they are constantly moving forward, the dragons look backward, symbolizing that the changes that the Wheel brings are seldom expected. Dragon designs have been utilized on medieval coats of arms for centuries and have even been traced as far back as 600 B.C., where they stood guard at the gates of the ancient city of Babylon.

"In keeping with the iconic theme, I used gothic greenman faces to represent the four immortal watchers, rendering them in a style reminiscent of the depictions of the four winds on ancient maps. The four rings, the four watchers and the two dragons total ten, in keeping with the numerological designation of the card."

XI

STRENGTH

XI. STRENGTH

Determination, irresistible will, the fortitude of character, courage, action, mind over matter, an ability to persuade others. Reversed: Weakness, timidity, despondency, an abuse of power, tyranny.

Divinatory meaning: Strength symbolizes a personal fortitude of mind, body and spirit. With the proper balance of physical strength, emotional discipline, intellectual determination and spiritual conviction, we can become invincible. Strength grants us the confidence and courage to confront life's dilemmas head-on. When times are trying, Strength will afford you the endurance to persevere. Be firm in your convictions and you will prevail. A show of force may be necessary to resolve the conflict at hand, but exercise self-control and restraint with the power you possess. By understanding your limitations and focusing your strengths, you will triumph. If this card is reversed, it signifies subservience and a weakness of mind, body or spirit.

A beautiful woman in a sheer silken gown balances on the stone ledge of an ancient tower. As she rises to meet the oncoming wind, her eyes are shut and her head is thrown back in ecstasy. At her side, a snarling gargoyle of rough-hewn stone glares menacingly downward at the world below.

Strength can manifest itself as physical superiority, as well as a strong will, emotional stability or a high level of self-confidence. Vargo deftly uses gothic symbolism to illustrate the various subtle aspects of Strength. Whereas the woman, delicately balanced on the brink of danger, exhibits poise, courage and self-confidence, the fierce beast at her side represents the power of physical force. True strength lies in the balance of knowing when to utilize force and when to exercise restraint.

Equally important is the strength of one's own character. Strength grants us the moral self-discipline to resist the temptations that surround us. This message of resistance is conveyed by the posture of the woman's body as she stands in defiance of the rising gale. Her billowing shroud conforms to the tempestuous wind, illustrating the concept that Strength allows us to bend without breaking.

The ferocious, wolf-like gargoyle that waits at the woman's beck and call depicts the primal beast that resides within us all. By properly directing our inner strengths we can understand how to keep the savage beast subdued and resist the urge to lash out with mindless, brute force. Strength also requires focused determination and will power to take a solid stance for your beliefs. This concept is illustrated by the gargoyle's rigid stone form as it clutches the ledge beneath him, granting him the fortitude to endure whatever tribulations may come his way. If a current situation requires you to take a stance on an issue, be strong and remain steadfast in your convictions.

Strength also creates a sound mental outlook and bestows us with an indomitable will. While we may not always be physically stronger than our opponent in a given conflict, by understanding our own limitations and channeling our strongest attributes, we can emerge victorious. When the spirit is strong, we can surmount any conflict or obstacle.

Another aspect of Strength, and one that should never be underestimated, is the power of persuasion. Although swift, forceful action can lead to a temporary resolution of a conflict, firm persuasion can often garner longer lasting benefits.

As the Wheel of Fortune turns to bring occasional turmoil into our lives, Strength grants us the ability to withstand and overcome any adversity we may face. Although Strength is usually perceived as an admirable trait, it can easily become a dangerous weapon when abused. It is important to remember that Strength should always be tempered with wisdom and compassion.

Artwork Title: Possessed (2001)

This painting was used in the *Tales from the Dark Tower* story "Vampire's Kiss," where the immortal spirit of the Dark Queen possesses the body of the newly made vampire, Rianna.

"Although the masculine form seems the obvious choice to symbolize Strength, a woman has traditionally been used to illustrate the concept in the Tarot," Vargo explains. "The common depictions show a woman taming a savage lion. Whereas the male associations with strength manifest themselves as physical attributes, the feminine ideals of strength are associated with fortitude of the mind and spirit. Keeping all this in mind, the previously existing painting *Possessed* seemed like the perfect image to represent Strength in the Gothic Tarot.

"Strength can be interpreted in several diverse ways. While some define it as a forceful action, others believe that true strength grants us the power to restrain from brute force. Since the concepts of Strength are quite varied, this painting emphasizes the physical contrasts between the two characters, symbolizing surrender and conflict, dominance and submission. While the woman faces skyward with closed eyes, the stone beast intently focuses his gaze on the world below, illustrating faith and determination.

"This painting also illustrates that might alone does not determine superiority. Although it is clearly evident that the gargoyle possesses more physical strength than the woman, the beast remains subdued by her grace and spirit, and there is little doubt as to who is the master and who is the servant."

XII

THE HANGED MAN

XII. The Hanged Man

Discerning, intuitive, heedful of consequences, making a self-sacrifice to acquire wisdom, learning from past mistakes, trusting in prophecy. Reversed: Narrow minded, bowing to peer pressure.

Divinatory meaning: Your image and outlook are on the verge of a dramatic transformation. The Hanged Man denotes that a period of withdrawal, inner reflection and self-sacrifice is required to attain a new level of awareness. When you find yourself at a standstill, use this time to reflect upon your life, then take the appropriate action to become the person you truly want to be. Have faith in predictions and follow the prophetic signs in your life. Let past experiences guide your future. New abilities and insights can be gained by subjecting yourself to difficult challenges. You will experience a period of tribulation, but you will emerge as a better person. That which does not kill us makes us stronger. If this card is reversed, it signifies selfishness, a weak will, conformity and limited vision.

A bat-like vampire with leathery wings hangs inverted, clinging by his clawed feet in an unnatural position of rest. His skeletal visage and cadaverous form denote that he is a creature from beyond the grave. At one time he was an ordinary man, but he has since undergone a drastic metamorphosis and the vestiges of his former self are now barely recognizable. His vampiric features remind us that he has relinquished his humanity to be reborn as an immortal creature of the night.

The Hanged Man is in the process of change, and he finds himself in a willing state of dormancy, meant to bring about spiritual enlightenment and physical improvement. He endures a period of self-sacrifice with the intent of achieving personal illumination or physical change.

The Hanged Man designates that an unavoidable setback has temporarily halted forward progress in our life, reminding us that by remaining calm and reflective, we can use this time to attain a higher state of consciousness.

Much like the Hermit, the Hanged Man has retreated from the outside world to concentrate his energies within; however, this creature isolates himself for the purpose of personal sacrifice to attain a higher level of existence. Like the metamorphosis of the larva to the moth, the mortal who sacrifices his humanity to become a vampire discovers that he must discard his former existence in order to complete the transformation into a more powerful being. He eventually evolves into a creature that truly expresses the persona that resides within his soul, thus realizing his ultimate potential.

This card also illustrates that we must exhibit patience and will power during a trial that will test the limits of our endurance. The Hanged Man calmly withstands his self-inflicted ordeal and emerges from it with newfound wisdom and power. He may seem to exhibit masochistic tendencies as he remains serene during his period of tribulation, occasionally deriving a sense of pleasure from it. He may also suffer to achieve a physical superiority. This may manifest itself as a strenuous workout routine or in the form of self-denial such as fasting or sexual abstinence.

The Hanged Man commonly appears to us during a period of stagnation in our lives, reminding us to use this opportunity to look at our current situation from a different perspective. Deep meditation may induce a mystical state that may temporarily increase your intuition and psychic perceptions. Intense soul-searching will lead to a better understanding of the personal changes we must make in order to achieve our desired goals.

The Hanged Man may also signify the end of a former identity, personality trait or lifestyle that we have outgrown. Let go of that which you have outgrown, and realize that you will receive far more in return as this new stage of your life develops.

Artwork Title: The Hanged Man (2002)

One of many paintings Vargo created specifically for the Gothic Tarot, the Hanged Man is not the handsome immortal of the Lovers card, but a bat-like nosferatu creature who has undergone a transformation from human to inhuman.

"I've gotten a lot of comments on this particular painting," Vargo relates. "Many people tell me that they find it disturbing, mainly because they perceive the image to be upside-down. Although it is an unnatural repose for a human, it is the natural resting position for a bat.

"The concept of the Hanged Man is one of serene meditation, ritual sacrifice and transformation. For this reason, I felt that a vampire in its demonic bat form, hanging inverted was the perfect image for this card. I had considered using one of my existing paintings, entitled *Vampire Hunter,* in which an inverted nosferatu creature hangs above the torch of a wary slayer; however, the distractions of the other elements in the painting took the focus away from the hanging vampire. Instead, I painted a new image that depicted a solitary, central character that was more in keeping with the Hanged Man's customary pose.

"Many traditional Tarot decks refer to the tribulations of Odin as the basis for the Hanged Man. In Norse mythology, the god Odin sought to gain the mystical runes, a magical alphabet of divination. Odin suspended himself upside-down from Yggdrasil, the World Tree, for nine days and nights in an effort to locate the runes, which were hidden in Mimir's Well at the roots of the tree. After plucking out his right eye and casting it into the well, Odin snatched the runes from Mimir, who let go of them long enough to claim the eye. Odin then bestowed the runes unto his mortal children, so that all mankind might benefit from his personal sacrifice."

XIII

DEATH

XIII. DEATH

An involuntary change of current circumstances, a transitory state, destruction and renewal, the lightening of a burden. Reversed: A fear of or a refusal to change, stagnation, lethargy, sleep.

Divinatory meaning: The Death card signifies the end of a current cycle in your life and the beginning of a new phase. A period of comfort and complacency will come to an abrupt close and you will be forced to adapt to the change. Destiny intervenes in your life to thwart your current path and present you with new possibilities. Be prepared to alter your course. Death symbolizes a time of drastic transitions and unforeseen changes beyond our personal control. A sudden and unexpected loss will force you to reassess your priorities. Destruction makes way for renewal, and endings lead to new beginnings. If this card is reversed, it signifies a standstill, monotony and a resistance to change, as well as health concerns and illness.

A wraith-like scarecrow stands beside a crude wooden cross in a barren, mist-covered field as a crescent moon looms overhead. A raven rests upon the figure's outstretched arm, signifying a dark omen of things to come. The scarecrow's other hand clutches a scythe, the tool of the Grim Reaper, who harvests mortal lives. His skeletal eye sockets are filled with an unnatural glow that echoes the blood-red sky behind him.

The Death card often fills our hearts with apprehension and fear as it seems to relay a grim forecast of catastrophic tidings. Within the Tarot, Death signifies that an end has come, but this end is not necessarily a bad thing and can often lead to bright new beginnings.

The scarecrow's red glowing eyes reveal that this creature is imbued with supernatural life that allows him to thrive, even beyond death. The raven, a traditional symbol of ill-omen, is also a carrion bird that feasts upon the dead, illustrating that death propagates life in the ongoing cycle of nature. Death, however tragic, is an essential part of the natural order of all things. Just as all life inevitably ends in death, we must remember that each ending makes way for new beginnings.

The bleak and desolate landscape of the artwork reflects the barren state of mind we may be thrust into when Death intercedes in our lives. Though a tragic loss is deeply felt, we must work through the pain and sorrow to carry on in the aftermath. The crude wooden cross marks a lonely grave, signifying that we should remember and respect that which has been lost, but we must ultimately move on, leaving the past behind us. While it is true that this card can appear when our lives have been touched by another's passing, the universal message is that the void in your life that has been created by the loss of a loved one can be filled with new relationships and experiences.

The Death card is represented by the fateful number 13, and the presence of the raven further illustrates the concept of Death being an ominous messenger. The Death card foretells that change will occur, and warns that we are powerless to stop it. Although this change may seem like a harsh dose of reality, the consequences may have beneficial effects in the long term. These changes often occur when we are most comfortable with our lives, forcing us to deviate from the safe path and venture into unfamiliar territory. This can be a frightening prospect, but it compels us to try new things that we may not have been receptive to in the past.

The Death card can also signify a change of spiritual conviction or personal outlook that often results from an emotionally devastating loss. Death is beyond our control, and this concept can either paralyze us with fear or strengthen our resolve to continue moving ahead. Death signifies that fate has redirected the path you have plotted for your future, presenting you with new choices and goals. Look at life's obstacles as challenges to be conquered, rather than insurmountable barriers.

Artwork Title: Scarecrow (2001)

For the Death card of the Gothic Tarot, Vargo considered other existing paintings, including several traditional style grim reapers, before deciding upon this more original and symbolic painting for his deck.

"Throughout the years," Vargo explains, "I have created several paintings that personify Death, but *Scarecrow* truly captured all of the connotations that are associated with this card in the Tarot. I combined various gothic concepts to create this image. The skeletal figure holds the scythe, the symbol of the Grim Reaper, and the slender curve of the blade is echoed by the crescent moon overhead. The withered branch, the tattered cloak of the scarecrow and the red sky further suggest autumn, the bitter season of harvest and death.

"In reference to Edgar Allan Poe, I utilized a deep scarlet color scheme to imply the Red Death and also incorporated the ominous raven that resides upon the scarecrow's outstretched arm. Since ancient times the raven has been viewed as a dark messenger of grim tidings, yet ravens and crows are scavengers that feed upon carrion, illustrating the concept that death creates new life.

"The Death card signifies an unexpected and drastic change that forces us to alter our current course in life. Most people slip into comfort zones with their careers and relationships, and although they may not feel content with their lives, they don't make any effort to change them. When fate thrusts change upon us, it compels us to work harder to realize our full potential and get the most out of life. In this way, a forced change can lead to the fulfillment of our most heartfelt desires.

"Death is also a stark reminder that we should make the most of things while we are still alive and that we should not take anything for granted. Live life to the fullest and you will have no regrets."

XIV

TEMPERANCE

XIV. TEMPERANCE

Patience and moderation, a frugal nature, justice balanced with mercy, action taken after contemplation. Reversed: Religious fervor, actions based on emotion, competing interests.

Divinatory meaning: Temperance signifies the blending of several diverse elements that work together to formulate a stable solution. Balance and unification are the key factors in attaining that which you desire. By utilizing a combination of small but precise doses, you can attain the best results. Skillfully combine your knowledge concerning the matter at hand with deliberate actions in order to successfully create your own resolution. Weigh all the factors at your disposal and determine how to combine them in the best possible way in order to achieve your goal. Gather your collected thoughts and focus them into a singular vision. If this card is reversed, it signifies an unbalanced disposition and principles that cannot be combined.

A black-caped sorceress pours a mysterious concoction from one golden goblet to the next before a massive cauldron of fire. As she stands within a mystic ring of crimson symbols, she appears to be in the midst of reciting a magical incantation.

The golden chalices she holds and the fiery cauldron before her illustrate the principles of alchemy, which grants her the power to unify the prescribed amounts of the diverse elements at her disposal. By utilizing the precise combination of spiritual strength, wisdom, knowledge and physical prowess, we can achieve perfection. Using the metaphor of a mathematical or scientific formula, Temperance allows us to assess the problems we face and determine what is required to balance the equation.

Temperance represents a unification of that which seems dual in nature. Twin wyverns stand back-to-back and support the blazing cauldron, symbolizing opposing forces that are united to achieve a common goal. A great deal of patience is often required in order to assess and combine the precise mixture of ingredients that counter and enhance one another. Certain properties that may be ineffective by themselves can create a powerful force when combined together.

Temperance teaches us to counterbalance opposite traits and mindsets in order to find the perfect medium. It is important to balance certain offsetting qualities such as justice and mercy, force and restraint, action and contemplation, compassion and discipline, in order to gain a healthy disposition and achieve our goals. By combining the proper mixture of these principles, we can attain our fullest potential. Balancing our spiritual ideals with our practical knowledge allows us to achieve personal harmony. By blending our dreams with the tangible materials and talents at our disposal, we can determine how to make our visions a reality.

Temperance also instructs us to use moderation, reminding us that too much or too little of anything can be ineffective. By being overly generous or too conservative with anything at our disposal, we may defeat our intended purpose. Temperance suggests a discerning and frugal nature, knowing exactly when enough is enough and also understanding that too much of a good thing can ultimately result in negative consequences

Aside from the important lessons it teaches, Temperance is also a symbol of healing, bestowing us with the skill to combine the resources that surround us into one unified vision in order to create the alchemical Elixir Vitae, or "elixir of life," which was said to have the power to cure all physical illness. As such, Temperance may relay the message that a mending process will begin as soon as we pick up the pieces of a broken dream, analyze which ones truly fit our plan, and reassemble them in the best possible way.

We are the sum of all of our knowledge and experiences. By mindfully unifying everything we have learned, we can achieve supreme balance and harmony.

Artwork Title: Sorceress (2002)

This painting was altered from its original version in order to make it coincide directly with the Tarot. Distracting elements such as a conjured bat and demonic wraiths were removed from the image and the two golden goblets were added.

"The traditional angel wings of the central figure were replaced by a black cape that suggests the wings of a bat," Vargo explains. "The elemental symbol of fire that appears in popular decks is dramatized by the flaming cauldron. The two wyverns that support the cauldron are symbols of conflict, and even though they stand directly opposed to one another, together they achieve a result that neither could attain alone.

"Many people have asked me about the possibility of a hidden message in the strange symbols that adorn the mystic circle. Although the characters were based upon the ancient Theban alphabet and the alphabet of the Magi, these symbols have no actual meaning and were designed purely as an artistic element to lend an air of mystery and mysticism to the piece. This also reflects the concept that alchemists created their own secret alphabets in order to encrypt their work in order to avoid religious persecution.

"Because Temperance dramatizes the mystical art of alchemy, I wanted the artwork to emphasize this ancient principle. Medieval alchemists were considered to be powerful wizards who believed that the ultimate combination of the four known elements would result in producing a magical fifth element known as Quintessence, which comprised the fabled Philosopher's Stone. This elusive artifact was believed to have the power to turn lead into gold and heal all ailments, making it highly sought after by ancient kings, even in a time when black magic and conjuration were deemed to be evil."

XV

THE DEVIL

XV. The Devil

An extraordinary effort is required to escape temptation, the dark side of human nature, selfishness, arrogance, sin, violence, struggle and oppression. Reversed: An overall weakening of moral fiber.

Divinatory meaning: The Devil represents the dark and oppressive forces that reside within us all. These unsavory aspects manifest themselves as psychological chains that restrict and halt our personal growth. Beware of self-destructive habits and mindsets that inhibit the ability to think clearly and act freely. Until new actions are taken, you will remain a captive servant of your fears and weaknesses. Free yourself from bad influences and realize that you and you alone are ultimately in command of your own life. Adversity obstructs your vision, making it difficult to clearly discern truth from falsehood. Temptation has led you down a dead-end path. If this card is reversed, it signifies laziness and a lack of ethics.

A great horned beast unfolds demonic wings as he stands upon a pile of human skulls. Two skeletons cower before him, shackled to their master by heavy chain leashes.

The goat-like legs and horns of the central figure depict him as a mythical satyr, in reference to the pagan deity Pan, lord of revelry and indulgence. This hedonistic connotation of the Devil reminds us that surrendering to our own temptations and vices may bring temporary pleasures but inhibits us from reaching our fullest potential to be productive in our lives. These vices hearken to the Seven Deadly Sins, which are listed as Greed, Sloth, Gluttony, Wrath, Lust, Envy, and Pride.

The Devil is also known as Satan, a name meaning "nemesis," suggesting a spiritual adversary. The two shackled skeletons enslaved by the Devil signify that we have become bound to a horrendous burden, stifling our spirit and making it impossible to continue on our current life's path. The Devil symbolizes petty fears and weaknesses that we allow to control our lives. These undesirable tendencies seem to rise to the surface from deep within us and can manifest as an addiction, depression, or any other form of mental obsession. As the skeletons bow in servitude to their dark master, he preys on their human weaknesses to gain power over their lives. By heeding his commands and surrendering to personal temptations, we relinquish our free will and allow the Devil to enslave our spirit.

The trappings of the material realm are suggested by the inverted pentagram that adorns the Devil's staff, signifying that our spiritual energy is channeled into selfish pursuits and material desires. The Devil raises his left hand to give the sign of sinister benediction as he stands atop a pile of skulls, symbolizing his self-indulgent nature and overall disregard for human life. Beneath his cloven hooves, a dozen skulls rest atop the twelve signs of the Zodiac, representing the Devil's power over all mortals. In reference to the numerical value of this card, the twelve skulls plus the three central figures total fifteen.

The Devil represents a malignant force that dominates us and keeps us from reaching our fullest potential. It may represent a destructive mental pattern, a bad habit or an undesirable personality trait that inhibits personal growth. Under the influence of the Devil card we experience a terrible sense of helplessness. If we submit to the Devil's will, we empower him, and in doing so, we have given up hope.

In ancient times the Devil was called the Great Liar. In this regard the appearance of this card warns that someone has made false promises and your aspirations have been based on lies. While under the Devil's influence, no addiction or obsessive need can ever be satisfied, yet we continue to listen to the darkest whispers within our own hearts, continually believing that they speak the truth. The Devil's lies cater to our own ego. By believing the lies we create the chains that enslave us, yet ultimately we possess the power to shatter those ties that bind.

Artwork Title: The Dark Gods (1996)

This card is a compilation of two of Vargo's works. The central demonic figure was taken from a larger painting called *The Dark Gods* and was then combined with a pencil rendering of the chain-bound skeletons that was designed specifically for this diabolical Tarot image.

"The original painting entitled *The Dark Gods* depicts four sinister deities standing side by side," Vargo reveals. "In this version, Satan stands with his left arm at his side and black feathery wings are folded behind him. After altering my rendition of Satan and combining it with other artistic elements, I created an image that represented the traditional Tarot depictions of the Devil.

"The diabolical personification of evil is an age-old concept. The biblical legend of the Devil has survived for thousands of years, portraying him as a fallen angel that has been reborn as the Prince of Darkness. The Devil reigns in Hell, where he punishes wayward sinners in the afterlife, but he also visits the physical world where he tempts mortal souls with material gains. The moral of this legend is clear—one moment of weakness can lead to an eternity of suffering. The Devil is a darkly intriguing mythical figure that has been a source of religious and literary inspiration throughout the centuries.

"The two chained skeletons stand upon the astrological signs of the Western Zodiac. Although their flesh has been stripped away, their gender can be determined by the astrological signs beneath their feet. The left figure resides upon the symbol of Taurus, signifying a male presence, while the figure on the right stands upon the sign of Virgo, signifying the female persuasion. The third astrological sign that completes the elemental triangle of earth is Capricorn, the goat, represented here by Satan.

"I intentionally chose not to use the color red while depicting the Devil, opting instead for the eerie green coloration of the artwork to lend an unsettling tone to the image."

XVI

THE TOWER

XVI. THE TOWER

Unexpected strife and upheaval, ruin, misery, havoc, adversity or disgrace, a sudden intervention of fate, the chance for a new beginning. Reversed: Oppression, imprisonment, tyranny.

Divinatory meaning: The Tower foretells that an unexpected twist of fate will have a sudden and dramatic impact on your life. The collapse of your stable surroundings will free you from the walls that you have built around yourself. A period of chaos will soon overwhelm you and your life will be subject to upheaval. An unforeseen turn of events will expose that which has been sheltered and the truth of your current situation will be illuminated for all to see. The Tower warns that the road you are traveling leads to disaster. The power of universal Karma strikes out to deliver what is justly deserved. A painful yet unavoidable truth must be reckoned with. If this card is reversed, it signifies a constricting force that confines the spirit.

A grim specter hovers between an ancient tombstone and a vigilant gargoyle in the misty dead of night. A massive castle stronghold looms in the background beneath the glow of a full moon, and a violent bolt of lightning streaks through the sky to strike the turrets of the keep's watchtower.

The Tower signifies dramatic change from an outside source that can radically alter your life's course. Unlike the thunderbolt of the Magician card, the Tower's lightning represents unbridled energy that can cause wanton destruction.

Like the Death card, the Tower foretells of disruptive changes. However, whereas Death signifies an ending that leads to new beginnings, the Tower manifests itself in much more unexpected and catastrophic ways, resulting in severely tumultuous effects on our surroundings.

The Tower does not signify mindless devastation, but instead represents an act of demolition that necessitates personal renovation and restructuring. The Tower also dramatizes that fate has caught up with us and will intercede in our lives in accordance with our past deeds.

The Tower warns of turbulent times that may shake the foundations of our faith. Although the spires of your dreams may be destroyed by this bolt out of the blue, you can rebuild that which has been lost, as long as your foundations remain strong. This rebuilding may make our lives better than before; however, we must be careful not to repeat the mistakes of the past. The concept of building a Tower so high that it attracts nature's wrath warns of the dangers of tempting fate and angering the gods.

Traditional depictions of people plunging to their deaths from the Tower's heights are replaced here by the wraith and tombstone, while the storm clouds and obscuring mist signify the chaos and confusion that the Tower's influence can inflict upon our lives. The rising moon and flash of lightning both signify illumination in the dark. These elements illustrate that the forthcoming chaos may shed light on the darkest aspects of our lives, allowing us to see the stark truth of a current matter.

The ominous stone gargoyles that stand guard over the castle entrance keep it safe from intruders, yet they can do nothing to ward off the unforeseen forces of the universe that strike from high above. This reminds us that even though we have taken great precautions to secure and protect our achievements, destiny can heedlessly invade and devastate our lives without warning.

The Tower also illustrates the consequences of being inflexible. When the destructive forces of fate intervene in your life, old habits and rigid mindsets will be shattered and therefore should be abandoned.

Although the Tower foretells of the destruction of our comfortable surroundings, it does not necessarily signify ruin. It may either suggest the time has come to relinquish our dreams of the past and move on, or that by reinforcing our convictions we can build a stronger future.

ARTWORK TITLE: HAUNTED KEEP (1998)

Vargo originally created this eerie painting as the cover art for the *Born of the Night* music CD, but later added the lightning bolt to match the traditional imagery of the Tower card.

"Decrepit old castles and haunted mansions provide the perfect gothic setting," Vargo relates. "The brooding phantom, weathered gravestone, menacing gargoyles, eerie mist and stormy night sky all contribute to creating a foreboding atmosphere.

"The shadowy specter is reminiscent of the dark figure depicted on the Fool card, but here he is much farther along on his journey. He has gained much wisdom and experience in his travels, but his journey is not complete. He now stands at the threshold of a fortress domain that holds great riches. Sixteen stone steps lead up to the castle entrance, in reference to the card's assigned numerical value.

"The Tower signifies a reversal of fortune that allows fate to punish or reward you for your past actions, causing you to feel the dramatic effects of the Karma you have created for yourself. As the external facade begins to crumble, the tower walls that you have built around yourself will fall away, and you will be exposed for the true person you are.

"The Tower illustrates the attributes and detriments of taking risks in our lives. We can either choose to reach for the heavens or remain comfortably grounded. High above, we are exposed to the lightning's fury as well as its brilliant illumination which pierces the surrounding gloom, while the safety of the ground below is shrouded in fog and darkness. If we take bold chances in our lives, we may attain lofty goals, but only at the risk of suffering devastating losses."

XVII

THE STAR

XVII. The Star

Hope and faith, a bright prospect, selflessness and sacrifice, one of a generous nature, renewal after loss or abandonment. Reversed: Pettiness, a patronizing or haughty nature, loss, impotence.

Divinatory meaning: The Star foretells that promising new opportunities are dawning on the horizon. The generosity of others will invigorate your spirit and revitalize your efforts. That which has been drained by battling adversity will be replenished. New hope is found after surmounting a period of personal hardship. The Star also acts as a distant beacon in the darkness that will guide you to your desired goal. Inspiration will come from afar and you will be motivated to follow a noble pursuit. You may be required to sacrifice your time or ability to help those in need. Give freely of yourself and you will be rewarded in kind. If this card is reversed, it signifies arrogance, ignorance and a loss of ability and drive.

A beautiful and radiant angel stands at the edge of a palatial precipice and pours rejuvenating waters from vases that she holds in each of her hands. As she empties the contents of one pitcher onto the stone pedestal beneath her feet, she pours the other into the clouds. Turbulent storm clouds brew in the background as a luminescent outline silhouettes a black star that looms overhead.

Traditional illustrations depict a maiden who empties her pitchers over land and water. The contents of one vase spills onto the stairs, signifying material matters, while the other pitcher pours into the clouds representing the spiritual domain. These are gifts of the conscious and unconscious realms. Both of these offerings trickle down to the Earth below, allowing her to impart her heavenly gifts unto the mortal world.

The Star is personified as a guardian angel who watches over us from above, bestowing us with spiritual gifts in our times of need. The column she rests against suggests the angel's heavenly kingdom, a place of lofty ideals and spiritual perfection. She distributes her gifts equally, bequeathing a balance of power between the conscious and unconscious, the spiritual and the physical. The angel's serene disposition grants her the ability to divide her attention and pour both pitchers with equal grace and ease.

The Star's bountiful offerings may manifest themselves as either a new opportunity, a winning mindset or material wealth, granting us the things we need to accomplish our most noble goals. The Star's charity is limitless, just as the unending streams that issue forth from her vases, as long as you return her goodwill upon those in need. Her example of benevolent generosity teaches us to utilize our gifts to selflessly give back to the world. The Star promises that by putting the needs of others before your own, you will receive even greater rewards in return.

The invigorating energy we receive from the Star revitalizes us when we are at the limits of our endurance, replenishing our spirit with a newfound drive that motivates us. Such rejuvenation grants us the ability to carry on, allowing us to attain things that were previously beyond our reach. When the Star bestows her gifts upon us, we are exposed to a realm of wonderful new possibilities. By shedding light upon the darkened world around us, the Star reveals new creative outlets at our disposal.

The Star tells us to have faith and comforts us in our darkest hours when we think we are alone and our hearts are filled with despair. The angel's soothing waters tame the brooding storm clouds that billow in the background, calming them and allowing the Star's illumination to permeate the gloom. The Star is a beacon of hope that shines in the night, helping us find our way in the consuming darkness that surrounds us before the dawn.

This card also reinforces the belief that wishing upon a star will grant your heart's desire. When the Star appears, it brings new hope in the form of opportunities that grant us the ability to make our fondest dreams come true.

Artwork Title: Peace (1998)

Altered from an existing painting which originally depicted a golden angel letting loose a dove upon the Earth, Vargo drastically changed the overall color scheme of the artwork, then added the pitchers and luminous black star.

"In creating the Gothic Tarot, my intent was to accentuate the shadow realms," Vargo reveals. "Since the Major Arcana required me to create artwork depicting radiant celestial bodies such as the Star, Sun and Moon, I was challenged to depict them in a way that conveyed a dark aesthetic. Although the outer edges of the star radiate a brilliant glow, the essence of the star itself is pitch black.

"Being affixed in the heavens, the Star embodies a force that watches over us, presenting guidance and illumination. This prompted the concept of personifying her as a guardian angel who bestows her gifts upon mankind from a kingdom in the clouds high above.

"The Star has always had close alchemical associations with the Temperance card and many Tarot experts consider them to be sister cards. I took this into consideration when creating the Gothic Tarot as well, depicting them as contrasting, yet kindred spirits. Whereas the Star is portrayed as a serene angel with white wings who calmly disperses the stable contents of her pitchers, Temperance is personified as an exotic bat-winged enchantress who sways rhythmically as she pours a mysterious concoction between her two goblets. The Star's color scheme is comprised of cold blues and black, while Temperance is depicted in volatile and fiery shades of orange and red. In addition, the angel inhabits a heavenly realm, whereas the sorceress seems to be sequestered deep in the shadows of the Earth.

"Although they have seemingly diverse dispositions, these sisters both strive to teach us the importance of attaining personal balance and equilibrium between the spiritual and material realms."

XVIII

THE MOON

XVIII. The Moon

The light and dark of life, secret fantasies, dreams tainted with nightmares, a poetic abandonment of reason, joy tempered with fear. Reversed: lost in darkness, error, deception.

Divinatory meaning: The Moon represents the dark and mysterious wonders of life. By following our dreams and conquering our fears, we can achieve our heart's desire. As a source of creative inspiration for artists, poets and musicians, the Moon sparks our imagination, allowing us to explore the realms of fantasy. New romantic prospects arise, opening our eyes to a realm of untapped possibilities. Wild passions may inspire temporary madness and impulsive behavior. Logic and reason give way to emotions. The Moon also symbolizes illumination in darkness and tells us to trust our intuition. If this card is reversed, it signifies a consuming darkness that misdirects our intended path.

A beautiful winged female reclines seductively in the luminous crescent moon. Her right hand reaches to caress the handsome dark angel who hovers before her. Devilish horns sprout from his forehead and his wings are ebony black, suggesting a dark and mysterious nature. Their longing and desire for one another is evident in their gazes, yet they remain separated by some unknown force. Four winged faces watch over the couple from the corners of the design.

The central figures of the Moon card embody the ideals of light and darkness. Though seemingly opposing forces, they share a passionate relationship with one another. Their contrasting dispositions offset and complement each other rather than clash. The male form, personifying the shadows of night, eclipses the moon as he draws near, consuming the light in his path. And though she is almost entirely engulfed in darkness, the Moon perseveres and beckons him closer with her irresistible charm. In this way, the Moon shows us the potent and near-fatal allure of dark desire.

Just as the Sun creates shadows during brightest daylight, the Moon brings illumination to the dark of night, allowing us to plumb the blackest depths of the abyss. Although we often fear what we cannot comprehend, the Moon allows us to overcome our apprehension when confronting the unknown. Those who seek to explore the shadows will discover secrets that will allow them to unlock the mysteries of our world.

The Moon's magic casts a romantic spell that has a deep, seductive allure. As a symbol of romantic possibilities, the Moon may signify that a secret admirer yearns for your affections from afar. In extreme cases, the Moon may represent infatuation or even romantic obsession.

Under the Moon's influence, temporary madness may take hold and impulsive behavior may cause us to act without thinking as we blindly follow our passions, heedless of the dangers that may lie in wait. While some may consider the Moon to be a maddening enigma, others find it to be a source of artistic inspiration. In this regard, the Moon can embody a creative muse or a healthy imagination that can serve to inspire the artist, poet or musician.

The Moon also represents the dark and mysterious wonders that await within our own dreams. These strange and fantastical visions are illustrated by the winged faces of the four dark seraphim that watch over the central figures. These faces depict the Satyr, governing the realm of hedonism; Medusa, who governs the realm of imagination; Azrael, who rules the realm of the dead; and the Moon beast, who presides over the realm of enchantment. As light and darkness merge, the children of the night arise from the four corners of night's domain.

The Moon has many phases, ranging from full illumination to complete darkness, which may signify deception or confusion arising from being misled. Trust in your powers of intuition and follow your inner voice.

ARTWORK TITLE: BORN OF THE NIGHT (1993)

This painting appeared in the *Tales from the Dark Tower* story, "Born of the Night," in which the personification of the dark of the Night and the light of the Moon unite as immortal lovers who spawn all manner of dark offspring.

"The moon has long been blamed for instilling madness in animals and people," Vargo relates. "The terms lunacy and lunatic are derived from the Latin word *luna,* meaning the moon. The gravitational pull of the moon also controls the tides, causing them to rise and recede during its various phases. Taking this into account, theories suggest that since the human body is mostly comprised of water, we may also be affected by the moon's power, especially during the full moon when its attraction is at its peak.

"The Moon card captures the dark essence of mystery and romance. While the muscular male form signifies dark desire, the delicate female form suggests irresistible allure. The moon goddess seductively beckons her lover forth, even though his dark wings eclipse her radiant light.

"Other Tarot portrayals of the Moon, showing crayfish and howling dogs, had nothing to do with the Moon's mysterious and romantic allure, only the madness associated with it. The artwork on this card hearkens back to earlier decks that depict a maiden reaching for her lover as he draws near to serenade her.

The Night summons like an unquenched love,
Beckoning with the promise of dark desire—

"As darkness descends and the moon looms in the sky, the children of the night rise from the shadows. Whether we believe in the Moon's magic or not, its attraction is undeniable. It has inspired people since the dawn of mankind and its influence continues to this day."

XIX

THE SUN

XIX. The Sun

Success, hope for the future, a fortunate marriage, the birth of a child, new opportunities and prosperity, stability, confidence. Reversed: fulfillment gained through effort.

Divinatory meaning: The Sun signifies a state of enlightenment that allows spiritual growth and grants illumination to see all things clearly. A new day has dawned and the fruits of your labors are blossoming. You will bask in revelation and all secrets will be known. Good fortune will shine upon you and you will reap great rewards. The Sun is a source of energy and vitality, bestowing spiritual strength and physical fortitude. You will not falter under pressure as long as you remain dedicated to your cause. The Sun also signifies a lasting union or marriage. Success is within your grasp. Have confidence in your own abilities and you will succeed. If this card is reversed, it signifies that your hard work will be recognized and appreciated.

A beautiful female angel draped in a sheer white gown is carried into the darkened heavens by her muscular bat-winged lover. Her head rests against his bare chest as he soars upward, cradling her in his arms. The shimmering crescent of a solar eclipse permeates the blackness behind them.

When the Sun appears, all things are basked in illumination. The Sun's majestic light reveals the truth of any situation, allowing us to see things as they honestly are. In this way, the Sun signifies a profound revelation that leads to a better comprehension of the world around us.

When shadows converge to obscure your path, the Sun's radiance shines on to permeate the foreboding gloom. Even during the consuming eclipse, the Sun pierces the darkness, illustrating that we have nothing to fear as long as a glimmer of hope remains. However, while you may be enlightened by the Sun's golden rays, you may be blinded if you stare directly into its brilliance for too long.

The tender relationship between the two central figures conveys a message of trust and devotion. The sleeping angel surrenders herself fully into her guardian's loving care and trusts him wholeheartedly, placing her faith in his ability to protect and sustain her as he effortlessly carries her upward to newfound heights. Unlike the lovers of the Moon card, who gaze intently into each other's eyes, the couple here face away from one another. While the female angel's pose suggests serenity and trust, the dark angel's disposition conveys his determined dedication to his cause. In this regard, the central figures illustrate the principles of contentment and ambition.

The Sun also signifies a solid union. This may materialize as a melding of ideas, a joint business venture, or a lasting marriage that can weather any storm and withstand the test of time. This concept is illustrated by the diverse natures of the angel and demon who share a blissful relationship. As weariness overcomes her, the female angel hangs her head and rests, while her partner carries on. His invigorated effort allows them to attain their lofty goal together.

The Sun's vital energy is the prime source of life on Earth. Without its light and sustaining warmth, we would cease to exist. The dawning Sun signifies a fresh start filled with limitless potential. Just as the nourishing rays of sunlight enable physical growth, the Sun signifies mental stimulation and growth of the mind and spirit, allowing us to reach our fullest potential.

The Sun is perhaps the most benevolent card of the Tarot. It is a symbol of glorious achievement that represents great joy and triumph. It is the embodiment of righteousness, purity and honesty. Representing the virtues of human nature, the Sun signifies the good things in life. It is also an omen of prosperity and good fortune. When this card appears, it denotes that your luck is at its peak.

ARTWORK TITLE: ECLIPSE (2000)

This compelling pencil rendering was adjusted for the Gothic Tarot. The dark angel's broad wings were cropped in to accommodate the dimensions of the card.

"As the fallen angel flies through the heavens on demonic wings, his dark essence eclipses the radiant sun," Vargo explains. "His lovely female companion rests comfortably in his arms, secure in the love that binds them. As darkness falls, night unfolds ebon wings to wrap the world in its dark embrace.

"Traditional Tarot illustrations of the Sun depict the couple as the twins of the Zodiac, but I chose to portray them as angels of light and darkness in order to continue the gothic theme of forbidden love exemplified by the Moon card. Whereas the Moon shows their mysterious and passionate attraction, the Sun illustrates the fulfillment of their union and devotion.

"Because the Gothic Tarot focuses on the beauty of darkness and shadow, the Sun presented the most challenging card of the Major Arcana. Since sunlight is the bane of vampires and other creatures of the night, it would have been virtually impossible to convey the virtuous connotations of this card by depicting it as a radiant orb. The concept of depicting the Sun as a solar eclipse provided a resolution to this dilemma.

"The sun has been a focal point in ancient mythology of various cultures. The Egyptian sun god, Ra, was worshipped throughout several dynasties. Depicted as a man with the head and wings of a falcon, he was believed to sail across the daytime sky in a golden ship. Each night he entered the underworld and remained there until dawn, when he was born again. The tears of Ra were believed to have spawned the first humans.

"The popular Greek myth of Icarus reminds us that flying too close to the sun will lead to ultimate doom. The ominous tale teaches us that we must be content once we have reached our desired goal and that greed will inevitably compel us to downfall."

XX

JUDGEMENT

XX. JUDGEMENT

Spiritual rebirth, accounting for faults and atoning for mistakes, giving and accepting forgiveness, a change or renewal. Reversed: Weakness, cowardliness, an unwillingness to accept change.

Divinatory meaning: The Judgement card signifies a time of personal atonement when you will be held accountable for your past deeds and transgressions. Your achievements and failures will be acknowledged and weighed against one another. Accept responsibility for all you have done and receive your penance. You will be required to adopt a new outlook on life. You must consider your past choices in life and answer for the decisions you have made. If you can forgive the indiscretions of others, you will be forgiven in return. Admitting your past mistakes and atoning for them will allow you to advance spiritually and move on. If this card is reversed, it signifies a reluctance to face the inevitable future.

A female spirit stands with her eyes transfixed upon the statue of a male angel who reads from a large book. As she silently looms among a field of ancient graves, tendrils of her gossamer gown waver in the breeze, caressing the tombstone behind her and fading into mist. The crumbling ruins of a cathedral archway can be seen in the distance, beyond the cemetery gate.

The Judgement card represents a time of personal soul-searching and atonement when we are held accountable for our past actions. Your efforts will be acknowledged and you will reap the deserved accolades. It is time to look deep within yourself and discover who you really are. If we can accept the truth of this intense scrutiny and criticism, we can learn to better ourselves during the next stage of our lives.

The beautiful specter who stands entranced seems to have been summoned forth from her grave by the angel's sermon. Her face conveys a sense of reverence and wonder as she listens to him read from the book he holds. It is the story of her past life, and the words he reads are etched in stone. Though our history cannot be changed, our future has yet to be written. Learn from the mistakes of the past, so that you do not repeat them. Though we have transcended this former life, we can learn from our past experiences in order to make wiser decisions in the future.

Judgement indicates that we stand at the threshold of a new stage in our lives and that we must look within ourselves to make necessary changes. Shed bad habits, let go of distressing memories, and move on without fear or regret. The cathedral ruins that loom in the background represent the crumbling remains of ancient history that should not be revisited.

The traditional artwork of this card is based upon the concept of Judgement Day, the time of reckoning when all souls must stand before the Divine and account for their deeds. Those who are deemed righteous and worthy are transported to Heaven, where they will reap their eternal reward. For only the just and penitent shall feel the rapture and be allowed to enter the heavenly kingdom, while the guilty shall suffer the consequences of their actions in the infernal regions of Hell.

Judgement also dictates that we must be considerate in our scrutiny of others and only offer fair and constructive criticism. We must also strive to be compassionate and forgiving of those who have committed offenses against us. Only by doing this will we gain the necessary closure that will enable us to progress in our lives.

Judgement precedes spiritual rebirth and regeneration. Reassessing our lives enables us to grow in a positive direction. Admitting our faults allows us to adopt a healthier attitude toward the shortcomings of others.

This card may also indicate that you will have to undergo a physical examination or a job evaluation. This card may also signify that you will soon be embarking on a venture into unexplored territory.

Artwork Title: Lector (1996)

The title *Lector* refers to the name given to one who reads sacred scripture to enlighten wayward souls. This painting was used in the *Tales from the Dark Tower* story, "Sorrow's End," to illustrate the tragic tale of a ghost who haunts the tower graveyard after falling victim to the whims of the Dark Queen.

Vargo explains, "Lector was the first of a series of paintings I created that explored the concept of a ghostly spirit who wanders throughout a graveyard, interacting with the various statues she sees each night. This theme was continued and carried over in the artwork for the Six of Cups, Eight of Cups, Six of Pentacles, and Nine of Pentacles as well.

"The idea that we may live on after death and return to revisit our earthly domain has been a popular subject for writers and philosophers throughout the centuries. Whether ghosts are truly restless spirits who have returned from beyond the grave to haunt the world of the living, or merely psychic impressions of the past, the presence of these supernatural entities has been documented by numerous credible witnesses. This evidence seems to offer undeniable proof of these phantom wanderers who haunt the shores of night.

"The Judgement card is also known as 'the Angel' in older decks which depict a heavenly being who sounds a trumpet to revive the dead on Judgement Day. I chose to replace the traditional trumpeting angel who wakes the dead and summons them forth from their graves with one who actually pronounces judgement upon them. Unlike the traditional depiction, the angel of Judgement in the Gothic Tarot is not a living being. He is only a sculpted effigy, but the lost spirit seems to be intently listening to his unspoken sermon, finding solace in his words."

XXI

THE WORLD

XXI. The World

Attainment and assured success, maturity, completion, signifies the end of a voyage or a change of residence. Reversed: Stagnation, a delay, a fixed state of being, isolation.

Divinatory meaning: The World card represents the end of your journey and the completion of an arduous quest. Your efforts will be recognized and rewarded and you will achieve all that you have worked for. The World is a symbol of fulfillment, perfection and universal enlightenment. Look at your current situation from a philosophical perspective. Accept and understand both sides of human nature, the light and the dark, chaos and order. You are the sum total of all you have experienced along your life's journey. Your mindset is clear and you now possess the knowledge, wisdom and ability to resolve the matter at hand. If this card is reversed, it signifies a narrow vision, loss of direction or extreme loneliness.

A crowned male figure commands two warrior angels who engage in battle with twin demons and their diabolic master. As the angels thrust their lances downward, the devils raise swords to meet them. A circular emblem rests between the two warring factions at the center of the design.

The World card signifies the completion of your journey. It represents realized potential and achievement of a lifelong goal. The World also signifies great success in all endeavors and fulfillment of our most cherished dreams.

The World card is all-encompassing. It is the embodiment of all of the forces of the universe, good and evil, order and chaos, light and dark. The imminent clash of angels and demons portrays the eternal struggle between good and evil that resides within each of us. Your personality becomes complete when you acknowledge these forces and allow them to maintain a balanced existence within you. In this way, the World represents your conscience.

The World embodies a unified conglomeration of all the concepts and elements that define our existence. Each person chooses the universal principles that suit their individual spirit and assembles them to create the world that surrounds them.

The forces of good and evil exist within the heart of every person. Their voices vie for our attention and influence the decisions we make in our lives. The breath that issues forth from the crowned figure's mouth carries the Divine word, the ultimate universal truth which created all things. In contrast, the forked tongue of the Devil connotes that his words are not to be trusted. He is a deceiver that tempts us to lead us astray from the righteous path.

The central ring, taken from the Realm Icon, represents a convergence of the diverse forces of the universe. It signifies the physical world, where the forces of light and dark intervene in the affairs of humans to sway their actions. The angels and demons that surround the ring are on the brink of combat, suggesting the inner conflicts that all men encounter when faced with a difficult decision.

The World advises us to look at things from an elevated perspective and to adopt a philosophical mindset. Look beyond outside appearances to see the inner truth. By looking at the big picture, we can understand how a current situation fits into the grander scheme. Profound assessment of all matters at hand will lead to a comprehensive solution. The World is not simply black and white. An overview of a current situation allows us to see the varying shades of gray that lie between. See the merits of action and passivity during various times and allow your experience to help you to determine the best route to take.

The World denotes a healthy mind, body and spirit, signifying that you have become a well-rounded and responsible person. You have reached a plateau in your life and all things are in order. This is not to say that your growth and progress has come to a halt, but only that you have achieved a significant stature. You have matured and now possess the experience, knowledge and wisdom to wholly obtain your goal.

ARTWORK TITLE: GOOD VS. EVIL (1999)

In the *Tales from the Dark Tower* story "Sanctuary," when gazing upon this chapel relief, the hero Brom relates, "There are forces of virtue, and forces of evil. With every breath they contend for the world, one human soul at a time."

"*Good versus Evil* depicts the eternal struggle between the forces of light and darkness," Vargo explains. "The Realm Icon, which adorns the backs of the cards of the Gothic Tarot, is an abstract representation of this image. The Realm Icon itself signifies 'order above chaos,' and the central ring symbolizes the earthly realm in which mortals dwell. In the Dark Tower mythos, the icon marks the tower as the earthly arena where angels and demons appeal to the mortal strengths and weaknesses of humans in an attempt to sway them toward good or evil. Though their voices compel us in different directions, our own free will grants us the ability to choose between the righteous path and the temptations of sin.

"Possessed of unearthly powers, these dark and majestic beings have existed since the dawn of time. Throughout the centuries, they have watched over the mortal realm with curious eyes and have had occasion to visit our world, inevitably becoming entangled in the affairs of mankind. According to legend, the Watcher angels taught mankind the forbidden secrets of magic. They were ultimately punished for sharing their mystical knowledge with humanity. Having been eternally banished to the mortal realm, the Watchers were said to have spawned all manner of dark and mysterious creatures.

"The laurel wreath and archangels that traditionally ornament the World card were replaced with a more balanced symbology to illustrate both light and dark, rather than focusing solely on the forces of righteousness."

The Minor Arcana

The Minor Arcana consists of 56 cards divided into 4 suits: Wands, Cups, Swords and Pentacles. The suit of Wands represents the energetic essence of fire, governing aspects such as creative energy, ambition, work and progress. The suit of Cups is likened to the essence of water, covering emotional and spiritual matters, love, relationships and intuition. The suit of Swords represents the essence of air, drawing connections to intellect, the force of will, communication and conflict. The suit of Pentacles is linked to the essence of earth for material and practical concerns including health and money. Each suit includes four Court Cards and ten Number Cards.

The Court Cards, consisting of King, Queen, Knight and Knave, generally represent people or certain qualities of a person's character. They may represent the person for whom the reading is being done (the inquirer) or a person who influences the inquirer. Male or female matters not, as a person may have character traits in common with either or both of the sexes.

The Number Cards illustrate various circumstances throughout one's life, such as joy or sorrow, failure or success, and they may be viewed as either a negative obstacle or a positive influence depending on their position in the spread. The Number Cards follow a logical order, with Ace representing the essence or main characteristic of the suit, as well as designating a beginning of some kind, and ten signifying a completion and the attainment of goals.

KING

WANDS

KING OF WANDS

Charming, wise and considerate, assured and confident, an honest and generous person. Reversed: Austere or severe in nature, a tendency to be arrogant, impatient and idealistic, impending danger.

Divinatory meaning: The King of Wands is wise, giving and honest. He is a charismatic host whose non-judgmental nature puts all guests at ease. By following his example and using our natural charms we can readily attain new goals and allies. The King of Wands represents a kind and generous benefactor who can instill a sense of confidence and trust. Have faith in your own abilities and you will succeed. Speak honestly with others and consider their needs above your own. If this card is reversed, it signifies overconfidence, restlessness, a feeling of superiority, or an omen of forthcoming danger.

Azrael, the Lord of the Dead, sits upon his ominous Gothic throne, wielding his arcane scepter of power. He is a gracious and hospitable host who quickly endears himself to all his guests. His calm and non-judgmental demeanor inspires a sense of trust rather than fear. Azrael's wisdom spans the realms of the living and the dead, granting him the power to foresee things in the physical and spiritual planes. He willingly shares his vast knowledge and insights with us and his generosity sets an example to be followed. Though confident and regal, he is never overbearing and does not force his opinions upon others.

Azrael's darkly majestic wings allow him to cross the threshold of the shadow realm and carry men's souls to the underworld. This somber task has endowed him with a natural sympathy for others. His honesty and integrity instills loyalty and fellowship wherever he travels. Although his unearthly appearance may seem foreboding, this guise symbolizes a spirit who does not need to cloak himself in elaborate finery or put on airs to demonstrate his noble intentions.

ARTWORK TITLE: AZRAEL (2002)

QUEEN

WANDS

QUEEN OF WANDS

Pure, loving and honorable, also harbors a desire for material wealth yet is practical. Reversed: Obliging, emotional, tight-fisted, also signifies jealousy and perhaps even deceit or infidelity.

Divinatory meaning: The Queen of Wands personifies devotion and honor. Her kind spirit makes those around her feel important, loved and needed. She takes comfort in life's luxuries, but she understands the significant worth and true value of her material desires. Be warm and considerate toward your close associates to ensure their allegiance and devotion. Your charm and honesty will draw others toward you, winning them over as loyal friends. If this card is reversed, it signifies someone who is overly emotional, jealous or dishonest, as well as someone who has been unfaithful or cannot be trusted.

A beautiful enchantress stands amid the ruins of an ancient site marked by the sculpted likeness of a wolf. A large black wolf-beast emerges from the shadows behind her to serve as her emissary and protector. She controls the savage creature with her enticing charms, and her hand rests lightly upon a human skull, suggesting her ability to control the fates of men as well. Her powerful spirit can tame others through gentleness and quiet sensuality rather than tyranny or force. Although her wolf companion snarls viciously, the queen stands with serene composure and dignity, confident in her charms and powers. She exerts a calming, mesmerizing influence, allowing her to win the loyalty of hardened hearts and tumultuous spirits.

Although essentially tender and reserved, the Queen of Wands possesses a dual nature that also enables her to be wildly ambitious. The deep scarlet color of her elegant gown suggests the fiery dimension of her character. Her material desires often manifest themselves as a hunger for life's riches, yet she is cautious not to spend her wealth frivolously.

ARTWORK TITLE: WOLF WITCH (2002)

KNIGHT

WANDS

KNIGHT OF WANDS

Well-liked, virtuous, energetic and headstrong, unpredictable, also an indicator of a departure or change of residence. Reversed: An indicator of danger, disillusionment, or an interruption of plans.

Divinatory meaning: The Knight of Wands represents the triumph of virtue over vice. His unpredictable nature grants him the ability to be spontaneous and carefree. He is determined, strong-willed and valiant. Use your intense strength of character to overcome obstacles and subdue any adversaries that may confront you. Be prepared for a sudden move or departure that may change the course of your life. If this card is reversed, it signifies a threat to your physical or mental well-being, as well as a distracting obstacle in your path.

A warrior angel in a gleaming helmet stands triumphant over a monstrous serpent that he has slain. He proudly clutches his imposing gilded staff in one hand while the other grips a golden shield. His intimidating physical strength denotes a combative spirit that seems more comfortable with dramatic displays of forceful action than quiet reflection and diplomacy. The iconography of an angel vanquishing a serpent is a classic representation of the conquest of evil. The peaceful blue sky that breaks through the turbulent heavens behind him further implies the triumph of light and virtue over darkness and chaos.

The angel's immense wings are tensed in preparation for flight once his foe is vanquished. An independent and free spirit, the Knight of Wands is not tied to any single place and can travel to the far ends of the Earth on a whim. His presence is welcomed by those he meets in his journeys and he is appreciated for his heroic integrity and willingness to hurl himself into action. Although his impulsiveness and occasional recklessness may be seen as flaws, his steadfast morals drive him to defend those in need.

ARTWORK TITLE: TRIUMPH (1991)

KNAVE

WANDS

KNAVE OF WANDS

An eager yet innocent lover, lively, positive and open, faithful, the bearer of unusual tidings, this person can possibly be a dangerous rival. Reversed: Laziness, instability, bad news.

Divinatory meaning: The Knave of Wands represents a loyal friend who can also be a formidable adversary. His liveliness and positive energy can become dangerous powers if the friendship falters. He is the bearer of unexpected news, perhaps of a romantic or financial nature. A new romance blossoms in your life or a former lover makes a surprise appearance. You will soon enjoy the benefits of financial security. Unexpected news leads to important revelations that impact your life in a positive manner. If this card is reversed, it signifies procrastination, erratic behavior and grim tidings.

A diabolical gargoyle clutches a skull in his right hand while his left hand grips a tall wand to stabilize himself on his stone perch. He displays the herald's scepter, signifying that he is a trusted messenger who brings unexpected news. The grim memento he grasps in his other hand is a reminder of his brooding power over men. The Knave of Wands is brutally honest and extremely loyal. However, if he were to become an enemy, he possesses traits that would make him a fierce adversary.

The Knave of Wands' message is of a personal nature, and it is most often beneficial and quite significant. His ferocious maw hangs open as if about to impart some crucial information and despite his devilish appearance, the fact that he does not possess a forked tongue indicates that he speaks the truth. This card can also represent one who is inexperienced in romantic pursuits but eager to learn the mysteries of the heart. Possessing a natural innocence tempered with devotion and loyalty, the Knave of Wands suggests a passionate partner in love's arena.

ARTWORK TITLE: DEATH GRIP (1999)

ACE

WANDS

ACE OF WANDS

Creativity, innovation and enterprise, a time of great activity, a beginning, a birth, fortune, inheritance, family matters. Reversed: Loss of imagination, decadence and ruin, a chaotic period.

Divinatory meaning: The Ace of Wands represents a time of enthusiasm and action. Proceed with your plans without delay, for there is no time like the present. This symbolic talisman also signifies a period of creativity that will produce wondrous results. This may manifest itself as the birth of a child or simply an idea that comes to fruition through your inspired talents. You may soon reap monetary rewards. The Ace of Wands is a regal scepter that signifies enterprise and respect. It is also a reminder of the importance of family. If this card is reversed, it signifies a conservative mindset or disastrous times.

A large crimson jewel surrounded by a pattern of inlaid gemstones adorns the top of an enchanted scepter. Embodying the essence of fire, this mystical wand of wizards inspires ambition and creativity. Ornate red flourishes decorate the background to illustrate the radiant energy that flows from the wand. In the proper hands this magical scepter can be a powerful tool, inspiring creativity that allows us to manifest our heart's desire. However, if the wand is misused, its powers can inflict disastrous results.

The wand's red gem signifies the mortal bloodline, stressing the importance of family and their unconditional support and devotion. Be considerate of the needs of your loved ones and take the time to improve a family situation. This arcane and mystical relic may also foretell of an addition to your family, such as the birth of a child. The Ace of Wands signifies that the time for action is now. If you have been considering your options in a pressing matter, do not waste time with further hesitation—make your move immediately and strike while the iron is hot.

ARTWORK TITLE: ACE OF WANDS (2002)

II

WANDS

TWO OF WANDS

Possessing strong will and high standards, indicates no marriage but a wealth of riches, physical stress, a decision to be made. Reversed: Surprise and wonderment, a willing acceptance of change.

Divinatory meaning: The Two of Wands signifies a strong and demanding character who expects much from those around him. A solid partnership will result in an increase of finances. Your strong will helps you achieve goals and attain leadership, but it can also intimidate others. You will have to make a difficult choice before you can move forward on your present path. New responsibility in your professional or personal life may cause pressure and strain, depleting your energy. If this card is reversed, it signifies an unexpected but welcome turn of events.

Two enchanted wands cross beneath a monstrous winged grotesque. The fiery gems that adorn the scepters symbolize strength and determination, while the gargoyle that presides over them is the emblem of the King of Wands. The pair of wands unite in a display of mutual support, signifying a solid and profitable partnership. The flourish design that decorates the wall suggests the wealth and prosperity that will result from such a partnership. However, this card also foretells of crossings in affairs of the heart, signifying an obstacle that prevents you from attaining romantic contentment. Although financial security may be within your grasp, the crossed wands and the solid stone wall represent a formidable boundary separating you from true love.

The Two of Wands also represents a crossroads in life that will present you with several options and require you to make an important choice. The diverse paths that are open to you are indicated by the ornamental engravings that point to the four directions of the compass. Do not allow your emotions to guide you at this time. Follow the voice of reason.

ARTWORK TITLE: TWO OF WANDS (2002)

THREE OF WANDS

Entwined and bound in an established trade or enterprise, successful commerce, exploration, a heroic deed that involves some self-sacrifice. Reversed: An end to troubles, a cooperative effort.

Divinatory meaning: The Three of Wands represents a contract that binds you to an ongoing project. A business venture may require a great deal of personal attention, but you will profit from your labors. You are deeply committed to your career and professional status. You will be involved in an event that will showcase your courage and strength, although it may come at a personal cost. New discoveries or journeys figure into your present circumstances. If this card is reversed, it signifies helpful deeds that lead to a reprieve from ongoing hardship.

A crimson serpent wraps itself around three intersecting wands, binding them together. The snake entwines himself throughout the wands, absorbing their mystical energy and channeling the power into constructive outlets. Reminiscent of the caduceus, the serpent-dominated emblem of the medical profession, the Three of Wands indicates the harnessing of combined powers for a profitable, creative purpose. The snake's intricate interweaving throughout the mystical scepters suggests a complicated, challenging venture that demands considerable skill and thought, but will ultimately prove worthwhile.

The Three of Wands is also a symbol of personal sacrifice that leads to productivity. Just as the serpent uses every fiber of its being to unify the wands and hold them together, we must realize that an extensive sacrifice of time or labor may be required of us before we can reap the rewards of our efforts. The Three of Wands may also indicate a dramatic ordeal in which one's valor and strength will be tested and some personal sacrifice will have to be made before victory can be achieved.

ARTWORK TITLE: THREE OF WANDS (2002)

IV

SERENITY + PROSPERITY + SANCTUARY + HARMONY

WANDS

FOUR OF WANDS

Joy and harmony, simple pleasures, peace and prosperity, achievement, enjoying the results of hard work, a willingness to share. Reversed: Continued growth and prosperity.

Divinatory meaning: The Four of Wands represents a harmonious union of mind and spirit. It signifies a time of peaceful tranquility, when we can enjoy a temporary rest. You will achieve a state of heightened serenity after attaining an important goal. The Four of Wands also denotes that you will be blessed with a period of happiness and prosperity. In matters of the heart, it suggests blissful fulfillment derived from simple gestures of devotion. If this card is reversed, it signifies that you will enjoy success as things continue to blossom.

A beautiful female ghost stands within the opening of an ornate archway as a full moon rises behind her. Four jeweled wands decorate the columns of her shrine and the words SERENITY, PROSPERITY, SANCTUARY and HARMONY are engraved upon the stone arch. Her monument offers a safe haven in a misty sea of unknown possibilities, allowing her a place of respite to temporarily enjoy the fruits of her labors. Her private sanctuary is a peaceful refuge where she can enjoy the simple pleasures of life with others who appreciate them as well. In this way, the Four of Wands represents a quiet celebration of prosperity spent with family or close friends.

The beautiful phantom and the full moon are perfectly aligned within the stone archway, illustrating that the material world, the spiritual realm and nature are in tune with one another at this time. The four columns that support the shrine further emphasize balance, cooperation and a harmonious union. Take notice of everything that surrounds you and allow yourself to appreciate the simple things that we often take for granted.

ARTWORK TITLE: GHOST AT THE GATE (1997)

V

WANDS

FIVE OF WANDS

Unavoidable problems and delays, petty annoyances, competition, a struggle for riches and fortune, with skill and foresight one may achieve their goal. Reversed: Conflict and probable betrayal.

Divinatory meaning: The Five of Wands represents obstacles that arise to obstruct your path. Anticipate unavoidable delays that will halt the progress of a current situation. Use this knowledge to plan an alternate route to reach your desired goal. Your perseverance will ultimately allow you to attain great things. The Five of Wands also represents a rival who has set their sights on your goal. Don't give in to the competition, let them inspire you to do better. If this card is reversed, it signifies disloyalty and hostility.

Grim specters bearing mystical wands rise from the shadows, blocking the road ahead. Ravens perch upon their arms, warning of darkness looming along the path you travel. The claustrophobic setting of the constricting shadows denotes unavoidable difficulties and problems closing in on a current situation. The mocking demeanor of the skeletal phantoms imply that you are at their mercy on this present path. The sinister, overwhelmingly hostile setting suggests that great caution should be exercised while attempting to pass through this troubled area. The arms and fingers of the skeletal wraiths form spiky, threatening branches, indicating a path that has become overgrown and fraught with hardship and delays, but these will only be minor setbacks if you maintain your focus on your goal.

    The five ravens and five skeletal phantoms leering in the darkness flank an ominous hooded entity who embodies an adversary who competes with you for a specific goal. Cloaked in darkness, this faceless foe signifies an unpredictable rival, shrouded in mystery, who stands directly in your path.

ARTWORK TITLE: SHADOWS (1999)

VI

WANDS

SIX OF WANDS

A messenger of good news, success and triumph, an optimistic outlook, a productive and energetic time. Reversed: Doubt, a pessimistic attitude, apprehension, fear of disloyalty.

Divinatory meaning: The Six of Wands represents someone who looks at the bright side of a situation, even in times of darkness and turbulence. Perseverance and determination under the most trying circumstances will lead to eventual victory. An optimistic attitude will guide you through great difficulty. You will receive good news during a time of duress that will ease your situation. The Six of Wands also signifies vibrant energy that leads to productivity. If this card is reversed, it signifies a negative outlook, fear and paranoia.

A fearsome wraith rides a steed black as midnight. Storm clouds billow behind the living nightmare and lightning streaks across the sky above. She holds a wand high overhead, as if to attract the lightning's power, and five more wands emerge from the swirling mist that surrounds the horse's hooves. Six bats rise from the clouds behind her, as if summoned forth to do her bidding.

The wraith's defiant demeanor in the midst of a threatening storm suggests a strong, energetic personality that is unshaken by negative developments. The rider seems to thrive on the turmoil of the setting, using it as inspiration. The surrounding storm provides a forceful energy that can be transformed and channeled into something positive and creative. The five grounded wands act as lightning rods to capture and disperse any untapped energy that may escape the wraith's scepter.

The Six of Wands is also a symbol of impending good news that will improve your life. The powerful stallion that has been harnessed by the rider allows her to deliver her message swiftly, before the full force of the storm can strike.

ARTWORK TITLE: NIGHTMARE (2000)

VII

WANDS

SEVEN OF WANDS

A time of consideration and discussion, a challenge to overcome, valour and fierce determination are needed to successfully achieve a goal. Reversed: Anxiety, indecision, a need for self-confidence.

Divinatory meaning: The Seven of Wands signifies a rigid mindset and determined outlook. Take a stance to face the challenges that surround you. Courage and strength of will enable you to overcome the obstacles on the road to your goals. Break free from the stagnant comforts of your everyday life and boldly explore new territory. Plan carefully before taking action and discuss your intentions with trusted associates. Be prepared to personally deal with any difficulties that may arise. If this card is reversed, it signifies stress, nervous tension and a lack of determination.

As an eerie mist engulfs the crumbling ruins of an ancient castle, a fearsome gargoyle comes to life. Although his immense wings are made of stone, he is determined to rise to the challenge and break free from his natural domain to join his brethren in flight. The creature must consider the consequences if he were to fail and fall, and weigh them against the benefits he would gain if he were to succeed. Bats take flight in the background, reminding him of the freedom that awaits if he leaves behind his stone confines.

Seven wands surround the gargoyle, providing him with the mystical energy that strengthens his will and gives him the single-minded determination to reach his goal. Though his face is turned toward the sky and his eventual freedom, the creature's right arm holds fast to the dilapidated pillar, suggesting a sense of caution and foresight to balance his ferocious courage. The weathered ruins remind him of the stagnation and hopelessness that will be his lot if he remains immobile and satisfied with his present situation.

ARTWORK TITLE: GRIMSTONE (2002)

VIII

WANDS

EIGHT OF WANDS

Making swift progress towards a goal, a hasty decision, a great amount of opportunities await, possibilities include love. Reversed: Disputes, a need to slow down and weigh options, jealousy.

Divinatory meaning: The Eight of Wands signifies rapid movement toward your desired goal. New opportunities arise that will expedite your mission. Be careful not to make any rash decisions in your haste. Several different options present themselves at this time. Numerous possibilities for romance surround you. Once your mind is set, do not hesitate to take action. You will quickly accomplish your present goals. If this card is reversed, it signifies halted progress, a disagreement or misdirected emotions.

A ghostly woman reaches outward as she swiftly advances down a gloomy corridor. She clutches a jeweled staff in her left hand as several more wands rise on either side of her. Although the scepters surround her, they do not impede her progress. The Eight of Wands signifies a period of speedy action when time is of the essence. Be cautious not to make hasty decisions in your hurry to reach your desired goal.

The surrounding wands represent the multitude of opportunities that lie in wait as you proceed along your current path. They may also signify new romantic interests that have risen. Although there are numerous possibilities, only a few of them prove to be substantial. However, you will not have the luxury of time to explore all your options.

The Eight of Wands signifies rapid progress in an ongoing venture. Quick thinking will be required to make fast-paced decisions. Keep a sharp mind, anticipate diversions that may lead you astray and be prepared to react to any sudden changes that may affect your established plan.

ARTWORK TITLE: APPARITION (1998)

IX

WANDS

NINE OF WANDS

Strength and determination to overcome obstacles, a true and pure purpose, a situation that is altered significantly with a solitary deed or bit of knowledge. Reverse: Obstacles, adversity and confusion.

Divinatory meaning: The Nine of Wands represents focused will power that enables you to triumph over adversity. A show of strength is required to break through personal barriers. Meticulous and deliberate action will produce long-lasting results. Efficiency and quality are the keys to success. Research the major factors of the matter at hand in order to attain an advantage. An unforeseen obstacle will alter your current plans. If this card is reversed, it signifies a period of adversity, disruption and chaos.

A seductive enchantress holding a jeweled staff poses before an enormous spiderweb and draws our attention to eight other wands that stand beside her. A red hourglass shape adorns her black corset, signifying that she is the widow of the web. Her endeavors and resolute intent have created a dreamcatcher that enables her to attain everything she requires to sustain herself. We can either look at the web as a barrier that restrains personal progress, or as a symbol of our own diligent labors that enables us to acquire all that we truly desire.

The Nine of Wands signifies that we have the power to overcome obstacles that deter us and we can attain that which we have labored for. A firm resolve will allow us to persist in our current quest, but knowledge is the key factor in the acquisition of our dreams. Study the main components of your situation and learn the best way to proceed. Examine all the resources at your disposal and determine the most efficient plan of action. Integrity and dedication will enable you to make your dreams become a tangible reality.

ARTWORK TITLE: BLACK WIDOW (2001)

X

WANDS

TEN OF WANDS

The trappings of success, fortune and gain come at a price, a burden to carry, oppression, a lawsuit may end in defeat. Reverse: Self-doubt, setting impossible goals.

Divinatory meaning: The Ten of Wands signifies material gains that are acquired at the expense of personal sacrifice and loss. A sustained effort will allow you to achieve wealth and status; however, the stigma of success may become burdensome. Someone in your life may be keeping you from reaching your highest aspirations. Investigate your suspicions to discover if they are valid. Be sure you have solid proof before making claims against someone who you feel may have wronged you. If this card is reversed, it denotes a lack of faith or unrealistic ambitions.

The ghostly form of a beautiful woman descends a castle staircase carrying a candelabra. Ten wands stand at the top of the stairs, while a fierce gargoyle sits perched below. The spirit cannot leave the magnificent castle that she inhabited in life and is cursed to haunt its darkened halls for eternity. Although the specter is barely more than mist, she is capable of carrying the candelabra, allowing her to light her way in the surrounding darkness. This enables her to explore the looming shadows and investigate her suspicions.

This card may also be seen as a sign of oppression, as the ten wands block the wandering spirit from reaching a higher level at the top of the staircase. Although the ethereal ghost may pass through this physical barrier, her candelabra cannot. If she chooses to venture forth, she will be forced to blindly explore this new plateau without the benefit of her illuminating light. The monstrous gargoyle that stands guard at the bottom of the staircase may thwart her from proceeding below as well. However, if she investigates closer, her light will allow her to realize that the sculpted stone figure poses no real threat.

ARTWORK TITLE: VIGIL (2000)

KING

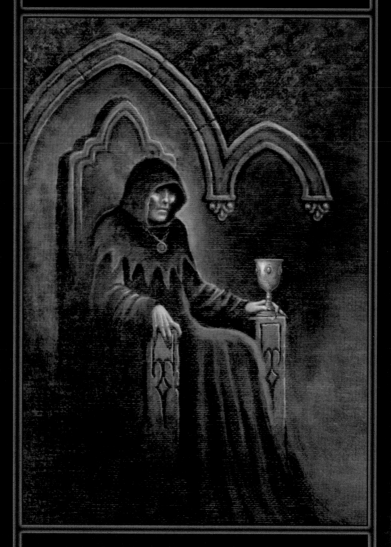

CUPS

KING OF CUPS

Mysterious and secretive, a negotiator, a professional in business or law, fair-minded, responsible, interested in art and science. Reversed: Prone to vice or injustice, may often conceal emotions, a rogue.

Divinatory meaning: The King of Cups represents a dark and mysterious persona. His interests in the arts, science and the occult may manifest themselves in seemingly magical ways. Revelations made in confidence should be kept secret. Demonstrate responsibility with the duties that have been entrusted to you. Be aware of the consequences that your actions may have on those around you. Maintain a mature and respectful attitude when dealing with others. If this card is reversed, it signifies sinister secrets, severe apathy, or a lack of will power.

An ancient wizard sits in his darkened throne room, sequestered in shadows and gloom. He holds a jeweled chalice in his left hand and wears an arcane amulet as a pendant. A practitioner of the forbidden art of alchemy, he possesses the mystical knowledge necessary to attain great things. The extensive breadth of his mystifying abilities teaches us to respect the wisdom of our elders. The darkness of his chamber and the shadows that mask his face indicate a person shrouded in secrecy and comfortable under the cloak of mystery.

As a master alchemist, the King of Cups has many responsibilities, and he contemplates them all very carefully. Sitting in thoughtful repose, he is clearly a man of deliberation rather than impulsive action. The wizard's hooded cowl suggests someone well-versed in scholarly pursuits and his solemn face is etched with the grave concern that he has for his subjects and practices. His stern countenance suggests one who is fixated on upholding universal truth and justice.

ARTWORK TITLE: KING OF CUPS (2002)

QUEEN

CUPS

QUEEN OF CUPS

Honest, gentle and warm, dreamy, a mysterious nature, intuitive, sensuous and sensitive. Reversed: Distinguished but not trustworthy, prone to vice or depravity, dwelling too much in a fantasy world.

Divinatory meaning: The Queen of Cups represents a perceptive and trustworthy advisor who possesses an exotic and mysterious allure. She is well aware of her sensuous charms and she uses them to her full advantage. Your physical appeal easily attracts others, but do not toy with the hearts of those who have fallen under your spell. Lend a sympathetic ear to a friend in need. Let your intuition be your guide when you feel lost or unsure. If this card is reversed, it signifies an unreliable person, a lack of ethics, or an unrealistic outlook.

An enticingly beautiful queen in a flowing black gown raises her goblet high overhead as an offering to the gods. Her tattered black dress and gothic crown are decorated with long thorns, suggesting that her delicate wisdom must be embraced gently and cautiously. She wears a dagger on her belt as a symbol of her uncanny ability to pierce to the heart of the matter with incisive accuracy and perception.

The Queen of Cups is an intuitive and sensitive soul who teaches us to trust in our own natural instincts. By following our inner voice, we can become more in tune with the mysteries of the world around us and better understand how to achieve lasting happiness. The regal posture of the queen denotes the refined, graceful spirit of one who has mastered the subtle art of seduction. She strides confidently forward, assured of her abilities and secure in the knowledge that she can effortlessly persuade others to fulfill her desires. The Queen of Cups is a mysterious and enchanting woman who shows us the importance of following our hearts to make our dreams become reality.

ARTWORK TITLE: MARA (1999)

KNIGHT

CUPS

KNIGHT OF CUPS

Graceful, sensitive, one questing for love, one who also has difficulty making a commitment, the arrival of an invitation or message. Reversed: Easily influenced, impractical, may indicate fraud or trickery.

Divinatory meaning: The Knight of Cups represents a forlorn soul who searches for true love. His mission is noble and pure, but he is also hindered by an inability to commit to one ultimate goal. In your quest for love, take care not to promise more than you are prepared to give. Current romantic pursuits may only garner temporary satisfaction. Expect the arrival of an invitation or a piece of information that could alter your current path. If this card is reversed, it signifies a gullible or deceptive nature, as well as someone whose ideas are immature or unreasonable.

A gaunt vampire stretches his clawed fingers over a trickle of blood that flows from the mouth of a diabolical grotesque. Standing before a weathered castle wall, the knight cradles a goblet in a distinguished manner, demonstrating etiquette and refined social grace. Though he is a darkly romantic figure who hungers for lasting love, he cannot completely give his heart to anyone or anything unless forced to. He stands posed with his back against the wall and avoids conflict by becoming one with the surrounding shadows.

The devilish gargoyle behind him seems to issue forth a message of pain and misery, but the knight attempts to shield us from the full suffering, as he intervenes to soften the harsh reality of the facts. The stream of blood denotes the grave arrival of some news or information with important repercussions. Though the gargoyle's nightmarish visage is menacing, his outstretched wings suggest a being that is more messenger than monster. Like the winged creatures of folklore, he travels solemnly between worlds bearing news that can change destinies for better or worse.

ARTWORK TITLE: DARK CRUSADER (2001)

KNAVE

CUPS

KNAVE OF CUPS

A quiet, studious nature, artistic or psychic inclinations, the bringer of news or a message, a time for meditation or reflection in personal life and in business affairs. Reversed: Deception, seduction.

Divinatory meaning: The Knave of Cups represents a calm and introspective soul devoted to artistic pursuits. Your intuition will lead you in the right direction during a period of uncertainty. A rumor may have dire ramifications, depending on its validity. A loved one's words may not match their actions. The truth lies somewhere in between. Intelligent analysis of the facts will enable you to resolve a pressing issue. A period of introspection and emotional restraint will allow you to see things clearly. If this card is reversed, it signifies misleading words and lustful seduction.

A forlorn gargoyle reaches downward from his lonely tower perch. As the stone creature strives to touch the mortal world below, a raven delivers an ominous message directly into his ear. A sculpted greenman face adorns the castle wall and a large goblet rests on a ledge before his open mouth to act as a receptacle for any wisdom that he may impart. The Knave of Cups denotes a time of careful consideration. We must decide if we should listen to the words that are whispered in our ear, or make the effort to seek the real story and partake of the full truth that lies within the chalice. This decision is best arrived at during a state of quiet meditation, when we remain isolated from the clamor of the everyday world.

Though he longs to be part of the realm below, the gargoyle clings to the stone wall behind him, unwilling to leave his perch until he is certain that he has made the right decision. The world beneath him is shrouded in mist, giving him further cause to reflect on his choice. The raven attempts to sway his decision by sharing wondrous tales of far away lands, while the graven stone face reminds him that this is where he rightfully belongs.

ARTWORK TITLE: OVERSEER (1999)

ACE

CUPS

ACE OF CUPS

Contentment, joy and abundance, harmonious home life, health, nourishment, a new relationship, truth in love. Reversed: Sadness, instability, troubled emotions, a false heart.

Divinatory meaning: The Ace of Cups signifies a replenishing of physical and spiritual energies. Partake of the abundant nourishing elements at your disposal. Eat, drink and relax in the company of those who bring you joy. A healing process has begun. You will enjoy a period of good health and physical prosperity. The Ace of Cups also foretells the beginning of a new friendship or romance. Open your heart to new possibilities. If this card is reversed, it signifies a time of solemn reflection, emotional insecurity, or a deceptive lover.

A solitary chalice ornamented with crimson jewels and artistic scrollwork signifies nourishment and healing of the body and spirit. Representing the elemental essence of water, the Ace of Cups signifies emotions, passions and spirituality. Romance is in the air at this time and a blossoming relationship should be nurtured. Traditionally associated with the Ace of Hearts in a deck of playing cards, the Ace of Cups may also be interpreted as a sign of true love.

The iconography of the goblet suggests the Holy Grail, which was believed to be a chalice of divine power that could replenish and rejuvenate the lives of mortals. This may signify that you have overcome a debilitating ailment or personal hardship and you will have no further worries concerning the matter. The Ace of Cups is a symbol of invigorating energy and love that allows us to rejoice in our own abundance. Now is the time to let your loved ones know how much they mean to you. True contentment comes from the realization of inner peace through the enjoyment of life's simple pleasures.

ARTWORK TITLE: ACE OF CUPS (2002)

CUPS

TWO OF CUPS

Cooperation and union between the sexes, love and passion, friendship, sympathy, in harmony with oneself and all of nature. Reversed: A false proclamation of love, a misunderstanding, a folly.

Divinatory meaning: The Two of Cups represents a harmonious union that leads to a period of bliss. This may include a business venture, a simple friendship or possibly a passionate love affair. Be sympathetic and attentive to the needs of those closest to you and you will achieve a binding rapport. Mutual interests lead to an exploration of shared desires. You are in tune with your surroundings and the ideas of others. A cooperative effort will garner much success. If this card is reversed, it signifies a foolish venture or a miscommunication.

Two jeweled chalices stand side by side below the graven relief of a winged guardian. A spell streams forth from the mouth of the lion-faced gargoyle, delivering a blessing of union and harmony unto both of the cups. Although the cups represent two separate individuals, they are bound by fate and now share similar desires. The winged lion motif suggests the heavenly Seraphim, who visited the earthly realm and imparted gifts of divine knowledge unto mankind.

The Two of Cups represents a state of synchronicity that has been achieved by two kindred spirits. Things are now in perfect harmony, as complementary qualities and talents now interlock to create a collaborative alliance. Just as the lion's face and eagle's wings in the gargoyle relief join to form a uniquely powerful new entity, the Two of Cups connotes a personal or professional marriage of contrasting powers, both aimed at a similar objective. The happiness and confidence that results from such a union will contribute to a positive outlook that will help in accomplishing mutually beneficial goals.

ARTWORK TITLE: TWO OF CUPS (2002)

THREE OF CUPS

The celebration, sharing and fulfillment of life, success and victory, merriment, a happy event, healing, solace. Reversed: Achievement, departure, independence.

Divinatory meaning: The Three of Cups represents a time of celebration when everyone involved in a successful project will reap the rewards of their accomplishments. An even dispersal of wealth and credit will lead to bountiful merriment and revelry. Combined efforts will allow you to attain great heights and gain a true sense of fellowship with your co-workers. The Three of Cups also signifies financial and emotional stability after a period of hardship and uncertainty. Problems of the past will no longer trouble you. If this card is reversed, it signifies a free spirit who has decided to move on.

A trio of jeweled chalices are stacked in a pyramid formation. Two of them form a solid and stable base for the third, which rests on top of them. This design symbolizes the lofty goals one can reach by working in cooperation with others. The trio also designates harmony of the mind, body and spirit, representing health, happiness and celebration. The twin pillars support a majestic archway, likewise illustrating the strength and solidarity that can result from the cooperation of separate elements working together.

As the top goblet is filled to capacity, its overflow is enjoyed by the supporting goblets below. This simple dispersal of abundance illustrates the principles of sharing our wealth with those who have allowed us to reach our lofty objectives. Although the topmost chalice has the enviable position of prominence, the three cups are essentially equal in size and importance. This illustrates that though public accolades are often given to the top-ranking member of a team, he would not have been able to attain this status without the combined contributions of his teammates.

ARTWORK TITLE: THREE OF CUPS (2002)

IV

CUPS

FOUR OF CUPS

Stagnation, a passive state, feelings of boredom and weariness, dissatisfaction with life, apathy, imagined troubles with no consolation in sight. Reversed: Novelty, action, new relationships.

Divinatory meaning: The Four of Cups represents a period of inactivity or boredom. Your productivity has been stifled due to a loss of motivation. A drastic action may be required before you are able to break free from the monotony of your everyday existence. You may experience a period of temporary disinterest when nothing seems to matter. The Four of Cups may also foretell that your problems will not cease until you take a critical look at the reality of your situation. If this card is reversed, it signifies a change of outlook.

Four chalices rest on an ornate ledge amidst a group of stone gargoyles. Although the gargoyles have been captured in various poses, they are all immobile and bound to their chiseled perch. While some are content, others yearn for change, yet the stone creatures cannot escape the stagnation of their ongoing existence.

The crowned gargoyle rests his arm and foot upon his companions, using them for support during a time of personal difficulty. Two of the topmost gargoyles sit in hunched poses, their wings folded behind them, suggesting that they are too timid and unmotivated to leave their perch. Their morose expressions are indicative of their listless, unfulfilled state of being. The winged gargoyle between them seems quite capable of taking flight, yet he clings to the ledge beneath him, unwilling to let go of the security of his current environment. His own inhibitions restrict him from seeking his dreams and realizing his full potential. The gargoyles face various directions as they search for an answer to their dilemma, yet none seem to acknowledge the chalices that hold the power that would enable them to break free from their present circumstances.

ARTWORK TITLE: GARGOYLES (1994)

V

CUPS

FIVE OF CUPS

A loss with something remaining, sorrow and regret but not without some consolation, a bittersweet inheritance or marriage. Reversed: New alliances, hopeful news, a return, affinity.

Divinatory meaning: The Five of Cups represents a bittersweet reminder of that which has been lost. A time of sadness will also have some beneficial merits. Cherish fond memories, but do not dwell in the past. Learn to appreciate the things that presently surround you and do not take anything for granted. Lessons of the past should be heeded, but do not allow them to dictate your future. Your accumulated wealth should be shared and enjoyed. If this card is reversed, it signifies hope and a return that reunites old friends.

A handsome necromancer ponders a human skull as a raven rests upon his arm. Five jeweled goblets are displayed on the shelves below his tower window. The starless night outside and the shadows that surround him suggest that his world is permeated by an oppressive gloom.

A necromancer is a wizard who has the power to speak with the dead. This unearthly ability grants him insights into the past, allowing him to benefit from the experiences of those who have gone before him. The skull he holds signifies his obsession with historical events. A reminder of a former time in your life may stir strong emotions. However, recalling fond memories may also bring a certain amount of sadness.

The jeweled chalices signify that he possesses a wealth of riches, but keeps it hoarded away, never allowing himself to enjoy all that he has acquired. While he is lost in the memories of the past, the raven attempts to draw his attention to the goblets, reminding him of what he possesses in the present. We must strive to appreciate the things we have in our current lives.

ARTWORK TITLE: NECROMANCER (2001)

VI

CUPS

SIX OF CUPS

Happiness and joy revisited in past memories, however, nostalgia brings only momentary bliss. Reversed: Looking to the future, a renewal, that which will come to pass, newly gained knowledge.

Divinatory meaning: The Six of Cups represents joyful reminders of the past. Heartfelt memories will uplift your spirit, but the sensation will only be temporary. Dwelling in the past results in unproductive distraction. A cherished keepsake will allow you to recollect and reflect upon a past moment captured in time. Mementos of a former period in your life will unlock bittersweet emotions. Remember the past with fondness, but live for the present. If this card is reversed, it signifies a discovery of important information, positive hopes for the future and renewed dreams.

A beautiful specter rests calmly on the steps of an ancient mausoleum. The spirit turns her back to the dark abyss of the crypt and seems at peace as she reads from a book, a memento of her former life. Six jeweled goblets rest on a lower step, but the phantom does not acknowledge their presence. The lone spirit clings to reminders of her past rather than enter the foreboding gateway, beyond which her destiny lies. Lost in joyous memories of her former life, she finds solace in her nostalgia, but the serenity she feels is fleeting and thwarts her from moving on.

A large cross covers the center of the gate and two angels are chiseled into the columns that flank the archway. The one on the left represents sleep, the Latin word *Somnus* engraved beneath it. The figure on the right is that of a winged skeleton, representing the angel of death, with *Mortem* chiseled below. Overhead a Latin phrase, *Noctem Aeternus,* meaning "eternal night," is etched above the archway, and a crown design rests above all, symbolizing the kingdom of the afterlife.

ARTWORK TITLE: NOCTEM AETERNUS (1996)

VII

CUPS

SEVEN OF CUPS

Imaginary and dream-like ideas, illusionary visions and fantasies lead to temporary and insubstantial choices, success in love. Reversed: Will, desire and determination are favored.

Divinatory meaning: The Seven of Cups represents dreams, imagination and visions that are conjured purely as escapism. Use your imagination and ingenuity to help you attain the goals that seem out of reach. Your creative notions may be misleading. Beware of fanciful or unrealistic ideas that can lead to folly and unwise decisions. The facts of a past situation may have been embellished. Heed the messages of your dreams. Romantic fantasies will come true. If this card is reversed, it signifies a strong desire to succeed, as well as elaborate wishes.

A beautiful maiden, the mythical Pandora, sits beside an open chest as spectral monstrosities and demonic creatures issue forth from the box, escaping into the night. Seven jeweled chalices rest upon the floor before her, but her attentions are drawn to the empty box as she appears lost in a state of dream-like reverie.

According to ancient Greek mythology, Pandora was the first mortal woman on earth. She was bestowed with a mysterious gift from the gods, a sealed box, with the instructions that she was never to open it. Eventually her curiosity overcame her and she raised the lid, releasing a flood of sorrow and strife to plague mankind. Pandora's tragic tale warns us of the dangers of succumbing to wild imaginings and making foolish choices based on our own selfish curiosity. Her expression is one of remorse as she realizes too late the dire consequences of her impulsive actions. Yet, when tempered with reason, unbridled imagination may also produce benevolent results, as when applied to artistic or romantic pursuits. In this regard, the Seven of Cups may also represent the fulfillment of our most provocative fantasies.

ARTWORK TITLE: PANDORA (1998)

VIII

CUPS

EIGHT OF CUPS

Rejecting good fortune, turning one's back on happiness, ignoring past concerns, dejection, timidness, modesty. Reversed: An abundance of joy and happiness, stability, feasting on life's rewards.

Divinatory meaning: The Eight of Cups represents rejection of that which is good and helpful. Take stock of the people and things that surround you and realize the benefit of embracing new ideas. Face your phobias, and do not empower them by surrendering to your fears. Do not be shy, reach out and accept the gifts that fate presents you. Step outside of your personal comfort zone and take a chance on new opportunities. Allow the world to see the real you, not just a glimpse of your outer shell. If this card is reversed, it signifies a wealth of material pleasures.

Eight jeweled chalices encircle an alluring specter who rises from the graveyard mists. She gently caresses the stone wing of a statue depicting the angel of death. She modestly turns away from the viewer, paying little heed to the goblets that surround her. Her disregard for the chalices has caused her to turn in the direction of the ominous graveyard monuments, indicating stagnation, loneliness and despair. The beautiful phantom teaches us that by turning our backs on the wondrous world around us, we cease to live, and merely exist.

Unlike this timid spirit, we should not let our inhibitions and fears prevent us from embracing the pleasures that are within our reach. Do not dwell in the gloom of the past when such bright and vibrant possibilities surround you. Utilizing the natural gifts and elements at our disposal will enable us to attain true happiness. Stifling our personal ambitions and turning away from the path to joy will lead to overwhelming sadness. Do not be ashamed to let others see you for who you really are. Only by facing the world can we truly allow ourselves to be seen in all our glory.

ARTWORK TITLE: SPECTER (2001)

CUPS

NINE OF CUPS

A good omen, satisfaction, sexual desires sated, physical and emotional fulfillment, success, renown, contentment. Reverse: Truth, loyalty and liberation, imperfections seem magnified.

Divinatory meaning: The Nine of Cups represents an omen of success and happiness. You will enjoy a level of fame that is worthy of your achievements. Share the abundant rewards of your labors with those who are deserving. You will be honored and remembered for your significant accomplishments. The Nine of Cups also signifies contentment and pleasure of the mind and body. Your emotional needs will be met and your physical desires will be completely fulfilled. If this card is reversed, it signifies trustworthiness and intense scrutiny.

Nine jeweled goblets are set above the obsidian sarcophagus of an Egyptian pharaoh. The Nine of Cups represents the fulfillment of our most passionate desires. The elaborate surrounding archway signifies the accolades of our success that will stand as a testament to our achievements for generations to come.

This image hearkens to the traditional Tarot depiction of a stately lord resting with folded arms beneath an arch of nine cups. Ancient Egyptian motifs are used in this image to represent a spiritual plane and arcane wisdom akin to the High Priestess. The sculpted sarcophagus lid depicts a crowned pharaoh who holds the royal crook and flail in his hands, denoting his high esteem. The goblets that rest above the doorway signify the wealth and abundance in our possession at this time. This may represent material gains, emotional prosperity or significant acclaim that should be shared with those who have contributed to our success. Allowing others to share in the glory of our accomplishments leads to a legacy of honor. In matters of romance, the Nine of Cups signifies complete fulfillment of our most intimate sensual desires.

ARTWORK TITLE: SARCOPHAGUS (1996)

X

CUPS

TEN OF CUPS

The heart at ease, a content family life, inner peace and tranquility, love, safety, completion, important interests being looked after. Reverse: A troubled heart, violence, fear, frustration.

Divinatory meaning: The Ten of Cups represents contentment and unconditional love. Tender devotion leads to a tranquil relationship. Your dreams of togetherness will be fulfilled. You will complete a goal that is very close to your heart. A break from your hectic routine will allow you to spend quality time with loved ones. The Ten of Cups may also denote a time of rest and healing. Relax and enjoy the quiet comforts of home and family. Rest assured that you will be properly cared for. If this card is reversed, it signifies emotional anguish or physical pain.

An enchanting succubus with demonic wings stands over her human lover as he lays unconscious. Ten jeweled chalices reside above the background archway, signifying a place of blissful contentment. The stone altar upon which the male figure lays is adorned with human skulls, suggesting the tranquility of the grave. The image of a bat sculpted into the stone of the central arch reflects the female's bat-like wings, designating this crypt as her home and private sanctum. The abundant chalices that adorn the crypt also denote the achievement of a personal goal that is very important. The healing properties associated with the suit of cups are amplified to their maximum potential, signifying that you will find peace and rejuvenation in a familiar place of comfort.

The Ten of Cups represents romantic stability and dedicated companionship. The pose of the two figures suggests that the female vampire may be bringing her lover across the threshold of death so that they may share a new immortal life together. This revitalization of spirit comes only after a duration of rest and transition. A serene period of relaxation leads to inner awakening.

ARTWORK TITLE: SUCCUBUS (2001)

KING

SWORDS

KING OF SWORDS

A strong and vigilant upholder of the law, a person in a position of authority, a powerful and commanding presence. Reversed: Very domineering nature, cruel and even barbaric at times.

Divinatory meaning: The King of Swords represents a champion of justice and the common good. Your opinion is highly valued and can be very persuasive in a current matter. Be resolute and stand behind your decisions. Honor your social obligations and attend events that you have been invited to. Your presence alone will be an inspiration to others. Do not abuse the authority that has been vested in you. Be mindful of the needs of those closest to you and act on their behalf. If this card is reversed, it signifies tyranny and savage actions.

A crowned warrior angel with black wings brandishes an ornate sword in front of a Gothic cathedral archway. The angel keeps vigilant watch over his domain, acting in the best interest of his subjects. He is an enforcer of justice and a sympathetic but honest judge of character. The central emblem of the Realm Icon decorates his belt, signifying that his jurisdiction does not exceed the earthly domain. An elaborate stone cross hangs from the central archway, signifying the righteousness of the warrior's cause. His relic sword further implies that he has the sacred power of the universe on his side, and he wields it with commanding authority. The angel's dark plate armor and black wings make him an imposing presence that demands a serious level of respect.

The King of Swords stands as a valiant protector of those who are unable to defend themselves, and he strives to ensure that justice prevails. He possesses a natural empathy for those who have been treated unfairly by life. Like this unearthly crusader, we should use our strengths responsibly, for the benefit of others, rather than our own personal gain.

ARTWORK TITLE: DARK ANGEL (1999)

SWORDS

QUEEN OF SWORDS

Private, self-reliant, sad or severe countenance, one who is quite familiar with sorrow or embarrassment, one accustomed to getting their way. Reversed: Prudish, deceitful, bigoted.

Divinatory meaning: The Queen of Swords represents a strong female who knows how to enforce her will upon others. Utilize the elements at your disposal to attain that which you desire. Do not allow emotions to obscure your vision. Stand firm in your convictions and remain resolute in your purpose. The Queen of Swords is also a solemn soul who has known much sorrow in her own life. Do not dwell in tragic memories or you will be consumed by grief. If this card is reversed, it signifies a reserved and conservative nature, dishonesty or prejudice.

A beautiful enchantress stands beside a nightmarish gargoyle atop an ancient castle ledge. The two dark souls revel in the night as they survey the world below. The Queen of Swords' solemn demeanor and somber black mourning gown reflects her inner sorrow. Her melancholy aura of moody reflection has turned her into an introspective figure who often isolates herself from the world around her. While sadness and heartbreak are unavoidable in life, we must take care not to let inner pain exile us from the world that surrounds us.

Consumed by her own wistful thoughts, the Queen of Swords may often enforce her will upon others. Her gargoyle companion, who stands ready to leap into action, will not be denied, suggesting the ferocious determination and power that the queen can unleash at any time. Although she has the winged beast at her command, the queen also carries a formidable sword, signifying that she is well-equipped to deal with any adversity. Despite her brooding tendencies, the Queen of Swords is neither weak nor passive, and she will not rest until she has achieved her objectives.

ARTWORK TITLE: UNLEASHED (2000)

KNIGHT

SWORDS

KNIGHT OF SWORDS

Clever, a skillful and brave warrior, ruthless against any opposition, war-like, destructive. Reversed: Impatient, boldly charging ahead, throwing caution to the wind.

Divinatory meaning: The Knight of Swords represents a relentless and resourceful warrior, hardened by past experiences. Remember the lessons learned from past conflicts and apply those strategies to your present situation. Show no mercy when dealing with your adversaries and do not allow betrayals to go unanswered. Be forceful and precise and strike directly at the heart of the matter. You may have to make an example of those who oppose you in order to win complete, unified support. If this card is reversed, it signifies an impulsive nature that inspires bold and reckless action.

A handsome warrior angel strikes a majestic pose as he gazes downward from his heavenly perch unto the world below. His right arm supports a crimson banner while his left hand firmly clutches a golden sword. The red banner attached to his gleaming lance suggests a herald of war and bloodshed. The angel's armor and confident demeanor indicate that he is unafraid of charging into the midst of a conflict and to do whatever is necessary to assure that justice is served in his dominion.

The Knight of Swords embodies the warrior spirit. Though the angel's sleek wings enable him to take swift action, his banner announces his intentions and gives fair warning of his arrival, allowing both sides of a conflict to make their peace before facing the indomitable force that will soon confront them. While the world beneath him may be consumed by turbulence, the angel stands at a vantage point that offers him sharp clarity of the situation as it unfolds before him. After formulating a calculated plan of action, his strength, experience and ability enable him to cut through the obscuring gloom to bring an abrupt end to any conflict.

ARTWORK TITLE: AVATAR (2000)

KNAVE

SWORDS

KNAVE OF SWORDS

Vigilant, perceptive, secretive and possibly deceitful, one who watches and waits for opportunity. Reversed: A more sinister aspect of these traits, also signifies unpreparedness or an ailment.

Divinatory meaning: The Knave of Swords represents a lurker in the shadows who waits for the opportunity to strike. Someone close to you may have ulterior motives and might be biding their time to take advantage of you. Be alert and watch out for any hidden agendas that may pose a threat to your plans. Take precautions to safeguard your plans and be careful who you trust. Someone may be standing between you and full illumination of the surrounding circumstances. If this card is reversed, it signifies immaturity as well as a dark and debilitating force.

An ominous gargoyle, silhouetted by the light of a full moon, sits perched atop a cemetery monument adorned with the graven image of a sword. His unblinking eyes shine with an unnatural glow, signifying that he keeps constant vigil over our world. His wings are folded behind him and he crouches as he guards the sword icon in an attempt to keep us from realizing the true extent of his power.

The Knave of Swords symbolizes one who watches and waits for the opportune time to spring into action. This may constitute advice for you to follow or may act as a warning concerning someone close to you. Safeguard your plans and be wary of whom you confide in. As the gargoyle watches from the shadows, his hulking form blocks the moon's illuminating light, further obscuring the fog-enshrouded landscape. This makes it exceedingly difficult to discern the correct path to follow. Do not blindly heed the advice of one who attempts to guide you. They may harbor their own motives to purposely steer you in the wrong direction. Tread carefully and stay alert as you progress into a new venture.

ARTWORK TITLE: NIGHTWATCHER (1997)

ACE

SWORDS

ACE OF SWORDS

Triumph, justice, power, conquest, a great force to be reckoned with in both love or in hatred. Reversed: The same but with disastrous results, also signifies conception or childbirth.

Divinatory meaning: The Ace of Swords represents the element of air, signifying intellect and active power. A combination of your mental and physical strengths will allow you to triumph in any conflict. A noble quest fills you with an undeniable sense of determination. Your achievements will be the result of a solo effort. You possess the power to forge your own destiny and nothing can hold you back. Do not allow this newfound power to corrupt your good intentions. If this card is reversed, it signifies the destructive forces of the human spirit.

A symbol of power and conquest the Ace of Swords is a potentially destructive force that can mold men's destinies. The honed steel blade possesses a double edge, suggesting that it can cut either way in any given situation. Just as it has the power to inflict pain and destroy men's lives, the sword also enables us to severe the ties that bind us and keep us from attaining our fullest potential. Though it represents the element of air, the blade was forged from the metals of the earth and tempered with fire and water, thus encompassing all the elements of the universe. This makes it a powerful force to wield, allowing men to channel their strengths through it. With the Ace of Swords in your grasp, there is no limit to the great things you can accomplish.

Many myths and fables utilize the iconography of the sword. Excalibur, the legendary blade that was bestowed unto King Arthur, granted him the power to rule his subjects with compassion and vanquish his enemies without remorse. Another fabled blade, the sword of Damocles, hung by a thread over the head of a seated man, so that he might comprehend the perils of being a king.

ARTWORK TITLE: ACE OF SWORDS (2002)

II

SWORDS

TWO OF SWORDS

An impasse, a stalemate, a conflict between like parties in which one or more may be blind to the truth before them. Reversed: Disloyalty, ill intentions or lies, a false identity.

Divinatory meaning: The Two of Swords represents a stalemate that cannot be resolved or negotiated. Realize that a present situation has come to a standstill. Proceeding ahead on your current course will prove to be frustrating and futile. Cut your losses and move on, but never let your guard down. A passionate debate will present opposing arguments that have equal merit. A new approach may be necessary to penetrate your opponent's defenses. If this card is reversed, it signifies betrayal, malice or someone who may be an imposter.

Two clashing swords form a skull and crossbones pattern beneath a crowned death's head. The crossed swords represent a conflict and their balanced positions suggest that both sides have come to a stalemate. The governing lord of death presides over the struggle in which one or both combatants may be unable or unwilling to see the true reason for the conflict, suggesting that blind faith and pride may lead to a fight without end. The winged skull also reminds us that men who cannot reconcile their differences peacefully have inevitably turned to war, seeking to settle matters on the battlefield.

The Two of Swords signifies an irresolvable argument or conflict of interests. All attempts to reach a mutual resolution have been unsuccessful and further attempts along these same lines will also prove to be useless. In such cases, it seems best to agree to disagree and move on. A mutual respect for one another will allow both parties to remain on cordial terms even though they share differing opinions. Stay steadfast in your convictions, but make an attempt to understand your opponent's point of view.

ARTWORK TITLE: TWO OF SWORDS (2002)

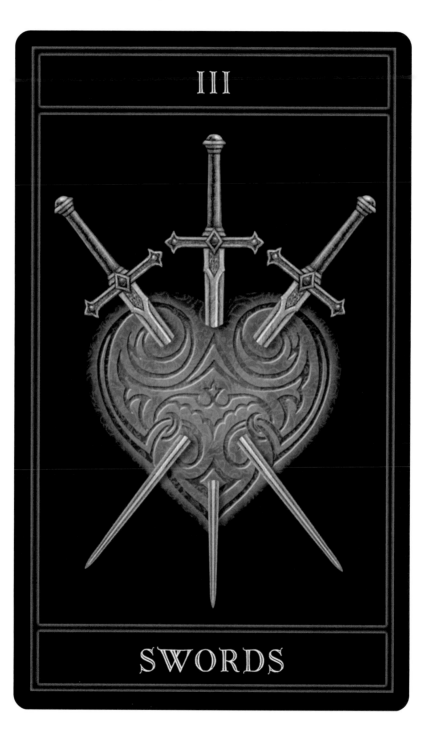

THREE OF SWORDS

A painful loss, a separation or absence, delay, removal or departure, rejection, betrayal, loneliness, grief. Reversed: Error, confusion, distraction, disorder.

Divinatory meaning: The Three of Swords represents misery or sadness brought on after a loss or separation. An obstacle will keep you from being with the one you love during this period and you may be forced to spend some time alone. Maintain a firm grip on your emotions and do not surrender to them. The Three of Swords may also signify a love triangle in which someone will be devastated. Romantic turmoil and disappointment may bring your spirits down. If this card is reversed, it signifies a disrupting force that causes romantic chaos.

A trio of longswords pierce the center of an ornate heart. Symbolizing painful emotions suffered at the expense of our own hearts, the Three of Swords foretells of emotional strife due to the loss of a loved one. The design illustrates a love triangle in which the emotions of three people collide while in the pursuit of love, or two or more suitors attempt to claim one heart. Such situations inevitably end in emotional disruption and abandonment. Do not allow your heart to govern your decisions. Though it may seem fragile, the heart is strong and enduring. While you may be entering a period of sorrow and pain, in time these wounds will heal.

The intricate labyrinth design that covers the middle of the heart suggests the complex, often confusing nature of romance. The pattern has no straightforward paths, as flowing curves intersect at abrupt, sharpened angles, demonstrating the hazards of attempting to navigate the realm of love. At the center of the heart, however, the winged icon indicates how we can eventually lift our own spirits above the distressing entanglements of failed love and free ourselves from its imprisoning maze.

ARTWORK TITLE: THREE OF SWORDS (2002)

IV

LIBERA ANIMAS OMNIUM FIDELIUM DEFUNCTORUM DE POENIS OBSCURUM

SWORDS

FOUR OF SWORDS

Exile, solitude, seclusion, withdrawal, a truce or rest during a dangerous period, make the most of this quietude. Reversed: Contemplation and organization of thoughts, wisely following advice.

Divinatory meaning: The Four of Swords represents a period of withdrawal for the purpose of rest. Put a halt to all strenuous activity and relax your mind and body. Retreat from a stressful environment to collect your thoughts. Avoid conflict at all cost. Remain calm and wait for a better time to act. Strive to find inner peace in your solace, and do not succumb to despair. Extreme introversion may lead to complete isolation from society. If this card is reversed, it signifies that the advice of a trusted confidant should be heeded.

This image of a beautiful female spirit leaning over a tomb with the graven image of a winged skeleton hearkens to the traditional image of a departed knight lying on a sepulchre. The Latin inscription on the sarcophagus lid reads "Libera animus omnium fidelium defunctorum de poenis obscurum," which translates to mean "Free the souls of the faithful departed from pain and darkness." This epitaph quotation suggests that this period of respite will enable you to conquer your sorrows and fears.

The Four of Swords represents an interim of seclusion and withdrawal during trying times. Whether this exile is self-imposed or enforced by others, it should be used as a time of rest, soul-searching and reflection upon your current situation. While the physical body is at rest, the spirit will also be reinvigorated.

Four longswords hang suspended within the archways that line the tomb walls, suggesting a time of truce when we should put aside our weapons. A disarming attitude may diffuse a potentially volatile situation. Retreat from any conflicts that may arise at this time and wait until the storm passes before taking any action.

ARTWORK TITLE: SEPULCHRE GHOST (1999)

V

SWORDS

FIVE OF SWORDS

Defeat or at best an illusionary victory, disgrace and dishonor is the price of such a conquest, infamy, degradation and shame. Reversed: The same, also signifies burial or funeral rites.

Divinatory meaning: The Five of Swords represents a disgraceful defeat at the hands of a ruthless adversary. A devastating failure leads to humiliation and sorrow. A sworn enemy will bring shame and ruin. Avoid being tricked into fighting a battle that you cannot win. Refrain from engaging in a present conflict and implement a dignified and graceful retreat from the situation. A vulgar display will reveal a sadistic nature. Do not allow yourself to be fooled by false hope. If this card is reversed, it signifies extreme cruelty and physical death.

A diabolical court jester sits upon the king's throne, gleefully displaying a sadistic memento of his rebellion. Five swords impale skulls upon the steps of the dais, signifying further atrocities and degradation inflicted upon the king's loyal subjects. The kingdom has been overthrown and madness and chaos rule.

Perhaps the most malicious card of the Tarot, the Five of Swords is an ominous harbinger of grim tidings. The mad jester exercises brutal measures to attain victory and cruelly flaunts his enemy's defeat. The crowned head upon the pike he holds is a shameful and vulgar display of the fool's triumph. Though extremely revolting, his barbaric and uncivilized methods act as a harsh deterrent against all who would dare to oppose him. When facing a vicious adversary who exhibits fanatical tendencies, it is best to avoid a direct confrontation. Trying to engage in battle against someone who callously employs such unscrupulous tactics may result in public humiliation. There is no shame in a graceful retreat and the minimal harm of a bruised ego is a minor concern compared to the embarrassment of suffering a devastating defeat.

ARTWORK TITLE: KING OF FOOLS (1992)

VI

SWORDS

SIX OF SWORDS

Leaving behind unsurmountable obstacles rather than attempting to tackle them again, emotions giving way to logic, possibly a voyage. Reversed: A confession, perhaps a declaration of love.

Divinatory meaning: The Six of Swords represents a present dilemma that cannot be resolved by a straightforward approach. A careful analysis of the facts will force you to relinquish your current pursuits in order to attain something more practical. A detour will allow you to circumvent an obstacle that cannot be directly overcome. You or someone close to you may soon be traveling afar. Look to trusted friends for help during this time of transition. If this card is reversed, it signifies a statement made in confidence or an admission of guilt.

An exotic enchantress stands on a small island, surrounded by a gloomy quagmire. A winged shadow beast, her loyal servant, waits at her side. She holds a sword in her hand and five similar blades can be seen emerging from the mist before her. The discarded swords stand as an ominous reminder of the fate of those who have tried to cross this barrier before. With the help of her winged companion she can safely retreat from her position, yet her attentions are drawn ahead as she calmly contemplates her situation. A skull at her feet suggests that she has no reason to stay on this spot. Either she has overcome a past adversary, or she has lost someone dear to her—either way, now is the time to move on.

The Six of Swords suggests that our fears can be conquered by analyzing a current dilemma and utilizing the choices at hand to find a logical alternative. A close friend can lend support and assist you in accomplishing your objective. A graceful retreat will enable us to conserve our resources for a new plan of attack. A roundabout approach may take more time, but it may be the only way to arrive at your desired destination.

ARTWORK TITLE: SWAMP WITCH (1991)

VII

SWORDS

SEVEN OF SWORDS

Using deceptive practices and cunning to achieve a goal, overly confident, a con-artist or thief, trickery may lead to one's own undoing. Reversed: Sound advice and instruction, also slander.

Divinatory meaning: The Seven of Swords represents a deceptive nature that may cause harm. Be wary of someone who may not be what they appear to be. Use caution in current business dealings and affairs of the heart. Be careful not to engage in any risky ventures at this time. An associate may have secretly created obstacles to keep you from reaching your goal. Someone you have confided in may take advantage of your trust. Do not take anything at face value, no matter how convincing it seems. If this card is reversed, it signifies a wise advisor or vile allegations.

A beautiful white-haired vampiress stands before an elaborate archway that leads into stark shadows. Her desirable form is human, but her arms end in bat wings, revealing a deceptive nature. Her pose suggests a welcome invitation to her domain, but her ulterior motives may not be in your best interest. She is a deceiver who uses trickery to gain your confidence and trust. Deception is also evident in the sinister shadows that conceal all that lies in wait in the archway beyond.

Seven ornate swords are displayed upon the staircase before her, obstructing her path. She exposes her wings to overcome this barrier, revealing her hidden nature only when necessary. The imposing blades also present a formidable obstacle to those who approach the beautiful seducer, indicating the severe danger that awaits those who foolishly attempt to enter her lair. The vampire's face is tilted arrogantly toward the heavens to suggest her powerful confidence and pride in her ominous revelation. The Seven of Swords warns us to proceed with caution in a current situation. Be wary of who you trust and heed your suspicions.

ARTWORK TITLE: CRYPT QUEEN (2002)

VIII

SWORDS

EIGHT OF SWORDS

A time of powerlessness and restriction, self-imposed censure, entrapment, bad news, also sickness. Reversed: An accident, treachery, possibly a fatality, opposing forces, difficulties.

Divinatory meaning: The Eight of Swords represents a time of inaction and helplessness. The circumstances of a present situation have pinned you down with your back against the wall. Unfortunate news may emotionally immobilize you until you can regain your strength and confidence. Prepare to remain in your current position until your spirits can be lifted. The Eight of Swords may also foretell of a debilitating illness that restricts your actions. If this card is reversed, it signifies a clash of ideas, betrayal and possibly death.

A beautiful spirit reclines against an ornate column. Her path is blocked by eight swords that have been thrust into the ground beside her. She assumes a relaxed position, as if posing for a portrait that may take some time to complete. Her delicate hand reaches out to steady herself against the supporting column, indicating a lack of physical or emotional energy. Her face is turned away from the hostile array of swords and the storm clouds that mount on the horizon, illustrating her inability to face the trying circumstances that surround her. This overwhelming feeling of immobility and helplessness may be self-imposed by a fear of confronting further hardship. Lost in a sea of fog and darkness, she desperately clings to the only security available. The debilitating gloom that surrounds her drains her resources, forcing her to rest and regain her strength before she can carry on. A lack of self-confidence during a stressful period may lead to a fragile emotional state. Be wary of those who would try to take advantage of you during this vulnerable time. Do not allow life's obstacles to overwhelm you. Compel yourself to take charge of your own destiny.

ARTWORK TITLE: REVENANT (1999)

IX

SWORDS

NINE OF SWORDS

Doubt and despair over problems that are mostly imagined, nightmares, anxiety, disappointment and regret. Reverse: Rational fears, shame, suspicion, imprisonment.

Divinatory meaning: The Nine of Swords represents haunting nightmares that plague your daily thoughts. Figments of your wild imagination fill your life with unnecessary tension and strain. Your worries will only serve to distract you from remaining focused on your goal. Do not dwell upon imagined fears, direct your attention toward tangible matters. Learn to accept the path you have chosen and bear the weight of your decisions without regret. If this card is reversed, it signifies apprehension, disgrace and incarceration.

A demon sits perched on the back of a stone gargoyle during a stormy night. Nine swords protrude from below, forming a barrier that separates the monstrous beings from the world beneath them. The unholy creature's eyes seethe with burning hellfire as he glares menacingly in the viewer's direction, stirring feelings of horror and dread. The Nine of Swords represents haunting nightmares and fears that weigh heavily upon us. This unwanted mental burden is often caused by paranoia and unnecessary worry over matters beyond our control. A stressful situation may cause undue anxiety that can distract our attention from truly important matters.

Just as the lower gargoyle seems incapable of flight while the demon remains on his back, the Nine of Swords signifies unreal fears that stifle our ambitions and keep us from making progress in our lives. The barrier of swords that restricts our fears from invading our domain illustrates that although our nightmares may seem horrific and threatening, they only exist in our minds and cannot affect us in the real world. Maintain your composure and attempt to turn your nervous energy into something productive.

ARTWORK TITLE: SANCTUARY (1998)

X

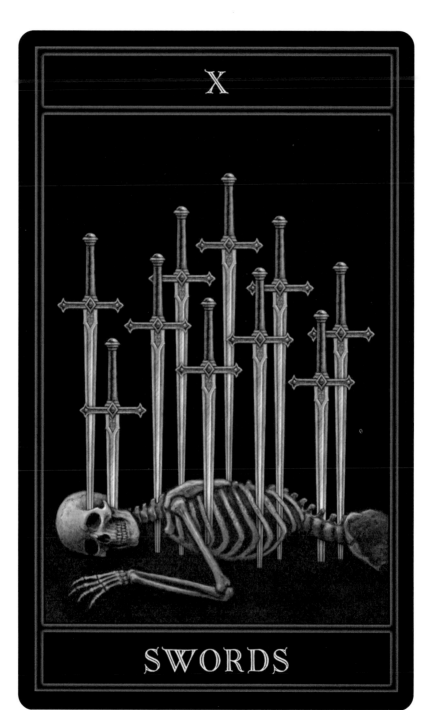

SWORDS

TEN OF SWORDS

A sudden and unexpected failure or disaster, pain, affliction, sadness, desolation, the result of an abuse of power. Reverse: Power, authority, profit and success albeit temporary.

Divinatory meaning: The Ten of Swords represents a dramatic turn for the worse in matters concerning health, love or business. Pay close attention to your present surroundings and be wary of any signs of impending disaster. Do not take the loyalty of your friends for granted. Act responsibly and treat those closest to you with the utmost respect. Although times are dark, do not despair. You will survive this painful time and emerge with a newfound wisdom. That which does not kill us makes us stronger. If this card is reversed, it signifies temporary gains and fleeting victory.

Ten jeweled longswords pierce the back of a skeleton as it lies in its final resting position. The Ten of Swords represents unforeseen disaster that can instantly destroy your plans and labors. This may manifest itself as a physical illness or a traumatic event such as a failure to achieve an important personal goal. It can also signify mental strife or sadness caused by the loss of a loved one.

The Ten of Swords also warns us to beware whom we trust. The fact that the skeleton has been stabbed in the back signifies vicious betrayal. An abuse of power may lead to a neglect of those closest to you. This may give rise to dissension that may ultimately end in harsh, rebellious action. Although the Ten of Swords may designate a time of great personal pain and suffering, it also denotes that you will endure this tragic experience and carry on with a strengthened spirit. This may pertain to emotional distress suffered after a difficult break-up that causes you to work harder to make your next relationship succeed. Do not allow this experience to crush your spirit. Make an attempt to take something positive out of it.

ARTWORK TITLE: TEN OF SWORDS (2002)

KING

ABANDON HOPE ALL YE WHO ENTER HERE

PENTACLES

KING OF PENTACLES

A leader who is dependable, valiant and loyal, somewhat imaginative and intellectual. Reversed: Prone to vice, perversity or corruption, possibly a warning of danger.

Divinatory meaning: The King of Pentacles is a valiant and noble leader who relies upon his own intellect and wisdom. He is an imposing ally who commands great wealth and power. His complex personality may be misleading, and he may seem to exhibit a brooding persona as he lends serious consideration to all factors in a given situation. He weighs both sides of a conflict and often sacrifices his own emotional needs for the greater good. If this card is reversed, it signifies a weakness of moral character and an omen of danger on the horizon.

A noble vampire lord stands among the menacing gargoyles that guard his tower domain. The pentagram symbol etched into the castle's stone facade marks his stronghold as a place that harbors mysterious forces and material wealth. The inscription on the tower wall reads "Abandon hope, all ye who enter here," an ancient warning that seems to mark the threshold of a grim domain. However, the King of Pentacles governs a realm of extreme self-confidence and faith, where mere hope is not enough to sustain our dreams. Do not rely on hope, but trust in your own abilities and be confident that you will succeed.

Though the external facade of his castle seems outwardly frightening, it shelters a wealth of wisdom and riches. The King of Pentacles is driven by an intense sense of righteousness and has cast his emotions aside for the greater good. In this regard, he may seem stern and unsympathetic as he stands as rigid as the stone creatures that surround him. Though he is bound by his duties and moral obligations, he yearns to follow his heart but refrains from surrendering to his human emotions and mortal weaknesses.

ARTWORK TITLE: DARK TOWER (1998)

QUEEN

PENTACLES

Queen of Pentacles

A practical nature, liberated, secure, intelligent, enjoying opulence and financial comfort, generous with gifts. Reversed: Sociable but suspicious and mistrusting.

Divinatory meaning: The Queen of Pentacles is a prestigious and ambitious woman who is driven to acquire great power and riches. Unrestrained by the conventions that limit the average person, she can rise to great heights to achieve things that seem unattainable. She does not allow others to deter her and often pursues eccentric routes to attain her dreams. She has much to offer and she bestows her gifts upon those whom she deems worthy. Although she is accustomed to a lavish lifestyle, she also exhibits a practical nature. If this card is reversed, it signifies a guarded personality or one who is detached and aloof.

An alluring vampire queen spreads her demonic wings as she stands before an ornate archway. A pagan pentagram is displayed behind her, signifying that she commands the mystical powers of the universe. The Queen of Pentacles represents a liberated female who is driven by her own lofty ambitions. She is wealthy and wise, passionate and strong, and although she respects the voice of reason, she harbors an insatiable thirst for power in the material realm. Though her methods are perceived as being unorthodox, her instinctive urges have led her to much success.

A woman of substantial means, the Queen of Pentacles is generous with her wealth. She often graces her loyal associates with her dark gifts, enabling them to share in her opulent lifestyle. Her vampiric wings enable her to rise to unimaginable heights, and as she rises, she is secure in her abilities to overcome any adversity and attain things beyond most men's dreams. Though she possesses a wealth of knowledge and intelligence, she may exhibit eccentric tendencies.

ARTWORK TITLE: DARK QUEEN (1999)

KNIGHT

PENTACLES

KNIGHT OF PENTACLES

A person whom friends can rely upon, patient, a conventional nature, responsible, eager to serve and able to endure hard work. Reversed: Slow, idle, lingering, placid, careless.

Divinatory meaning: The Knight of Pentacles represents a reliable and focused person who is perfectly suited for his assigned tasks. He is a diligent worker who takes his mission very seriously and exercises thoughtful discretion. Secrets shared with a trusted associate will be kept confidential. The Knight of Pentacles may also deliver a message of good fortune and act on your behalf. A personal emissary will keep you safe from harm. If this card is reversed, it signifies someone who takes little pride in their work.

A brooding white-haired vampire stands before the crumbling ruins of a pagan cathedral. His foot rests upon a discarded human skull as he strikes a somber pose. Three wolves stand at his beck and call, ready to heed their master's commands. His pale complexion suggests one who keeps to the shadows, and his black cloak further implies a discreet, secretive and clandestine nature.

The Knight of Pentacles is a trusted and dependable ally who takes great pride in his work. He is an intelligent and calculating individual who forms a strategic plan before making any moves. Once his course of action has been plotted, he labors diligently to accomplish his mission. He may also relay a message of good news that will have a major impact on your life.

The Knight of Pentacles also offers a sense of security and protection. The skulls that lay at the roots of the withered tree suggest scandal that must be quashed before it can do harm. The fearsome wolf pack represents kindred spirits that share a like mindset and will not permit anything to stand in their way. With the Knight of Pentacles at your side, you will have no worries.

ARTWORK TITLE: LORD DRAVEK (2000)

KNAVE

PENTACLES

KNAVE OF PENTACLES

An overseer, hardworking, meticulous, studious and diligent, a positive omen of forthcoming news and messages. Reversed: Fickle, too serious at times, a harbinger of unfavorable news.

Divinatory meaning: The Knave of Pentacles represents a diligent guardian who watches over you. A close associate is looking out for your best interests and may intervene in a current situation to act on your behalf. Recognize and appreciate the efforts of those who have offered vital assistance and support. Heed the advice of a trusted friend. The Knave of Pentacles may also signify a servant or messenger. You will soon receive much anticipated news. If this card is reversed, it signifies a grim message.

A winged gargoyle keeps eternal vigil from within the shadows of a gothic alcove. The mysterious inscription etched into his pedestal is written in the ancient Alphabet of the Magi. The letters translate to "GOLEM," designating him as a magical servant who has been imbued with unnatural life to do his master's bidding.

The Knave of Pentacles represents a close associate, generally an educated and hard-working person, who comes forward to serve your best interests. Someone who is under your influence has a great admiration for you and highly respects your opinions. A trusted overseer will allow you to dedicate more time and thought to attaining your goals. Delegate your authority to others who will execute your plans without fail.

The Knave of Pentacles can also signify an emissary who relays messages between you and distant partners. The golem's monstrous wings allow him to cross between the physical world and the spirit realm to deliver insightful information that may affect your destiny. This news traditionally relates to financial opportunity or the direct acquisition of wealth.

ARTWORK TITLE: GOLEM (2000)

ACE

PENTACLES

ACE OF PENTACLES

Material comfort and financial security, fortune and good luck, contentment, high levels of intelligence, physical and mental well-being. Reversed: Great riches bring corruption.

Divinatory meaning: The Ace of Pentacles represents the elemental essence of earth, signifying the attainment of material wealth. A sudden windfall will bestow great rewards. Your finances will be secure and all your material needs will soon be be met. Good fortune shines upon you. You are blessed with the intellectual and physical abilities that will enable you to achieve great things. Your luck is at its peak at this time. You will enjoy an abundance of all you desire. If this card is reversed, it signifies misfortune and greed.

A talisman adorned with an upright pentagram is set against an intricate design of blood-red flourishes. The five points of the pagan star signify the four elements of earth, air, water and fire, as well as the essence of the spiritual plane. The pentagram design itself seems to be woven from one continual and interlocking shape, representing the binding of the elements of the universe. This arcane emblem is often used as a mystical circle, within which magical spells can be worked. In this regard, the pentagram empowers the supernatural abilities that reside within us.

The suit of Pentacles is also known as coins in other Tarot decks. This designation connects this suit to material wealth and financial gains, denoting that you will enjoy the comforts of good fortune. You will be blessed with gifts that will grant you a true sense of inner worth, enabling you to accomplish your goals with ease. The Ace of Pentacles is also a sign of irresistible attraction and romantic success. The object of your desires will fall under your seductive spell and will be unable to resist your charms. Now is the time to enact your dreams.

ARTWORK TITLE: ACE OF PENTACLES (2002)

II

PENTACLES

TWO OF PENTACLES

Recreation and celebration balanced against minor troubles and frustrations, the arrival of news or a message. Reversed: A false display of merriment, an exchange of letters.

Divinatory meaning: The Two of Pentacles signifies a social celebration that allows you to free your mind of your daily burdens. You will enjoy your time but you may also experience minor irritations and setbacks. A hectic schedule may force you to juggle more than one job. Disperse your time more evenly between your daily responsibilities and the pursuit of your dreams. Recreational activities may enable you to mix business with pleasure. A message will give you personal direction that will allow you to make an important choice. If this card is reversed, it signifies an insincere facade and written news.

A devilish gargoyle face supports two pentacles that hang from chains suspended by his horns. The diabolical sculpture does not maintain an equal balance, as the pentagrams hang at uneven levels. The suspended pentacles signify two separate callings in our life that we cannot decide between. In such cases, one often takes precedence over the other, making it difficult to maintain an equal balance between our obligations and our dreams. A crack in the stone wall between the two mystical symbols represents minor troubles that may arise but will not cause any significant harm.

The Two of Pentacles represents a festive time to celebrate the good things in our life. The gargoyle's horned head is reminiscent of the Greek god Pan, the lord of revelry and indulgence. This serves as a reminder that, while moderate celebration may lift our spirits, too much wildness will ultimately lead to an abandonment of our responsibilities. Partake of a leisurely activity that enables you to take your mind off of your worries, but do not allow it to interfere with your personal obligations.

ARTWORK TITLE: TWO OF PENTACLES (2002)

THREE OF PENTACLES

Glory and recognition attained through skilled labor or a trade, artistry, a rise to noble ranks, aristocracy. Reversed: Pettiness, mediocrity, feelings of envy, disapproval.

Divinatory meaning: The Three of Pentacles signifies an attainment of recognition for your talents and efforts. You will be honored and praised for a major accomplishment and your work ethic will instill a sense of pride in all those around you. The acclaim and renown you earn for your expertise and achievements will bring new opportunities your way and enable your to reach a loftier place in society. You may be required to leave you personal mark in a prominent place before you can achieve your true destiny. If this card is reversed, it signifies jealousy and rejection.

A trio of ravens perch upon a castle ledge above the sculpted likeness of a woeful harlequin face. Three pentagrams are chiseled into the wall behind them, designating this spot as a place of material wealth and mystical empowerment. The ravens have attained a lofty objective and reside in a place of honor that signifies their achievements. The coveted ledge beneath them may also serve as a launching point that will enable them to reach even higher goals.

The Three of Pentacles signifies a deserved financial reward or career promotion that elevates us to a venerable rank. The graven image of the court jester that adorns the prestigious heights of the castle's walls illustrates how the lowly fool has risen to a place of esteem. An artistic display of your skills will earn you a distinguished reputation. You will discover a realm of heightened opportunities once you have made your mark on society. This may manifest itself as the signing of a legal document, such as a contract that enables you to attain success and great wealth.

ARTWORK TITLE: WOE (1991)

PENTACLES

FOUR OF PENTACLES

Gifts, legacy, inheritance, an attainment of wealth or power may lead to greed, possessiveness, spoiling. Reversed: Waiting and wanting for more, being kept in suspense.

Divinatory meaning: The Four of Pentacles represents great rewards that are bestowed upon us. Enjoy the trappings of good fortune, but do not be blinded by greed. Realize the true value of things that money cannot buy. Indulgent behavior may lead to temporary bliss, but it may also have unwanted repercussions. Though you may be blessed with abundance, remember to take everything in moderation. Material possessions mean little if you have no one to share them with. If this card is reversed, it signifies insatiable desires and prolonged anticipation.

A beautiful woman shrouded in a black gown and cape gently caresses the chin of a sinister gargoyle. Four pentacles decorate the stone wall beside her and a goat-horned satyr adorns the ledge beneath her feet. The Four of Pentacles signifies the abundance and possible abuse of material possessions. You may benefit from a windfall that will instantly bestow great wealth upon you. Although you may be able to afford a richer lifestyle, do not be led astray by the temptation to surround yourself with unnecessary extravagances. The monstrous gargoyle who sits perched upon the highest ledge signifies the ugliness that can result from being spoiled and having every whim satisfied, illustrating how too much of a good thing can have negative results. The woman's voluptuous bosom and the howling satyr beneath her feet suggest the excesses of physical gratification and carnal pleasures. Such indulgences may temporarily satisfy your wanton urges, but feeding these dangerous desires will only allow them to grow stronger until they ultimately become uncontrollable. Taking things in moderation will allow you to enjoy life to the fullest.

ARTWORK TITLE: BELLADONNA (2002)

V

PENTACLES

FIVE OF PENTACLES

Destitution in matters of money or favors, impoverishment, financial ruin and material losses, despair and embarrassment. Reversed: More of the same to a somewhat lesser degree.

Divinatory meaning: The Five of Pentacles signifies loss and despair. Prepare for a possible turn of events that may devastate your life. Your current circumstances provide little security for you and those who are dependent upon you. A period of hardship may force you to adjust your lifestyle. Do not gamble with your future. Conserve your resources until your situation improves. Set your mind on getting your finances in order and work diligently toward this goal. If this card is reversed, it signifies difficult times and financial adversity.

A loathsome vampire lurks among the ancient tombstones in a misty graveyard. The remnants of a cathedral archway stand in the background as a testament to the former glory that once resided here. The skeletal remains of the graveyard's occupants litter the foreground. Their bones have been picked clean by scavengers, leaving nothing for the predators that feed upon flesh and blood.

The Five of Pentacles represents hardship and destitution. A loss of material possessions and any means of support will make it difficult to sustain hope, but do not allow yourself to be discouraged. This period is only temporary. Endure whatever is necessary as you wade through this difficult period and you will eventually emerge from these troubled times. Withered branches, scattered bones and crumbling gravestones further signify hardship, decay and ruin, and the dense fog that obscures the surrounding landscape makes it difficult to see beyond the pervading gloom. The vampire's tattered cloak and hunched posture suggest his humbled state. Maintain your focus on getting through this period of hardship and you will persevere.

ARTWORK TITLE: NIGHTSTALKER (1990)

VI

PENTACLES

SIX OF PENTACLES

A clearing of debt, repaying favors with kindness and generosity, sharing the wealth and good fortune with others. Reversed: Desire, envy, the illusion of security, squander.

Divinatory meaning: The Six of Pentacles represents a fair and even dispersal of wealth. Share your good fortune with those in need. The time has come to repay old debts. Personal favors are valued more than money. Your past indiscretions will be forgiven if you are sincerely penitent. An honest display of your emotions will allow others to understand your true feelings. A genuine offer of fair reimbursement will be openly accepted. The gift of charity is always welcome. If this card is reversed, it signifies greed, jealousy, false security, or one who spends wastefully.

A beautiful female spirit clutches the robes of an angel statue that stands within a misty graveyard. Two tombstones, each adorned with a trio of pentacles, stand at either side of the statue. The angel's outstretched hands seem to signify forgiveness while also gesturing toward the six inscribed pentacles, as if offering the gift of charity. Just as the statue appears to forgive the repentant spirit, we should forgive old debts and offer second chances to those who have made an effort to mend their ways. Likewise, debts owed to others should be repaid in some manner.

The Six of Pentacles signifies reimbursement and a fair dispersal of funds to help those in need. A financial dispute may result in a lawsuit if you make no attempt to settle things fairly. The humble ghost, her head bowed, represents a person brought low by circumstance who beseeches someone for help. By aiding those suffering from great hardships, we will lift their spirits, ensure their loyalty, restore their dignity and enable them to improve their situations in the long term. As a result, they will one day be able to return the favor when we are in need.

ARTWORK TITLE: SORROW'S END (1998)

VII

PENTACLES

SEVEN OF PENTACLES

An invitation to act upon, not a time to rest on past achievements, complacency may lead to failure, success is assured only with diligence, ingenuity and hard work. Reversed: Anxiety about finances.

Divinatory meaning: The Seven of Pentacles represents the threshold of opportunity. Accept an invitation to partake in a new venture. An untrodden path will lead to intriguing new possibilities. Do not pass up the chance to explore unconventional ideas and see things from a different perspective. Maintaining a dedicated work ethic will garner great results. Old accomplishments are no longer impressive and may eventually be forgotten. The time has come to begin a new project. If this card is reversed, it signifies stress and worry over money.

A ghostly watchman dressed in Victorian garb beckons you to step inside the wrought iron gate that surrounds a dilapidated gothic manor. The decrepit condition of the mansion implies that without proper maintenance, our past achievements will decay. A dense fog covers the scene, signifying that you are entering a realm of uncertainty. A stone gryphon perched upon the gatepost stands watch over the entrance to this domain, signifying that only invited guests will be permitted access to the exclusive opportunities within.

The Seven of Pentacles symbolizes renovations that must be made in our life in order to improve it. This can suggest a change in our attitude, personal appearance or productivity. New opportunities will allow you to reinforce your reputation. The exploration of an unconventional path will lead to the discovery of several new creative venues. Even though this unfamiliar path may be difficult to discern and navigate, remain focused and keep moving forward in a steadfast manner. It is time to build and improve upon the accomplishments of the past.

ARTWORK TITLE: DARKLORE MANOR (2001)

VIII

PENTACLES

EIGHT OF PENTACLES

Craftsmanship, skill and business savvy pay off, turning hobbies and interests into a profitable endeavor, gainful employment or a commissioned work. Reversed: Vanity, overly ambitious.

Divinatory meaning: The Eight of Pentacles represents artistic skill that enables you to create wondrous things. Take the time to hone your craft and develop your natural talents. You will be given the opportunity to exhibit your prowess and capitalize on your abilities. Your ingenuity and expertise will be put to good use. A constructive application of a pastime will lead to great profit. With enough persistence, a hobby could become a career. If this card is reversed, it signifies a self-absorbed person who is overly concerned with their own appearance.

Two chiseled gargoyles keep eternal vigil from their perch high overhead. Beside them, an elaborately sculpted column is adorned with eight pentagram designs, displaying the artistic skill of an expert craftsman. The intricate detail of the gargoyles and pillar stand as a testament to the great artistry and expertise involved in sculpting the stone. Whereas the gargoyles serve as mere decorative ornamentations, the supporting column is both practical and aesthetically pleasing. By serving two functions, the sculpted pillar illustrates how an artistic skill can be utilized in more conventional applications, and thus be capitalized upon.

The Eight of Pentacles denotes that, with persistence, we may develop an enjoyable and creative pastime into a successful and profitable business. A skillful creation that transcends the boundaries of artistic expression may result in new career opportunities. While one gargoyle clings to the stone rail before him, the other spreads its wings and prepares to take flight, illustrating that we can either remain stationary and keep our dreams to ourselves or allow them to take us to new heights.

ARTWORK TITLE: SENTINELS (1998)

IX

PENTACLES

NINE OF PENTACLES

The benefits of a discerning and prudent nature are realized, the enjoyment of finalizing a grand accomplishment, safety and financial security. Reverse: Deception, mistrust, an unfinished project.

Divinatory meaning: The Nine of Pentacles represents the celebration of accomplishing a major goal. Be cautious and wary of all that surrounds you. A great amount of perseverence is required to reach the objective you have set. Your mission will soon be complete and you will reap the satisfying rewards of your labors. Stay on the safe path and proceed slowly but deliberately toward your goal. Do not take any unnecessary risks that might set you back. If this card is reversed, it signifies work that is incomplete, as well as devious behavior.

A lonely specter visits a forsaken and neglected grave in a small forest clearing. A raven sits perched upon the overgrown tombstone and seems to convey a message to the beautiful ghost, keeping her attentions focused on her goal. A great deal of concentration and effort is required to penetrate the dense thicket of trees that surround the remote site in order to reach the small clearing. Such an undertaking requires intense scrutiny and fortitude of spirit. The tangle of vines that entwine themselves around the headstone hold it firmly rooted, keeping your goal stable and secure, while the raven helps to guide you through the surrounding wilderness. Your individual talents and steadfast labors will enable you to accomplish your objective with great competence and attain a substantial reward.

Nine pentacles form a festive arc above the scene, designating a time of celebration and enjoyment once you have reached your goal. By not taking any foolish risks or detours, we are able to find our way without suffering any pitfalls or setbacks. Careful contemplation and deliberate action will lead to great rewards.

ARTWORK TITLE: THE FORGOTTEN (2000)

X

PENTACLES

TEN OF PENTACLES

The fruition of a lifetime's worth of hard work, financial and emotional security, the support of family and stability of home. Reverse: A loss, theft, losing to games of chance, a dowry or pension.

Divinatory meaning: The Ten of Pentacles represents the attainment of your most cherished goals through painstaking effort. Rest assured that your dreams will come true. Relax within the familiar comforts of your home environment. Surround yourself with the people and things that bring you joy. Those you have entrusted are looking after your best interests. The stability of loved ones will sustain you in a time of need and will carry you through any difficulties. If this card is reversed, it signifies a loss of material gains or prestige.

A brooding vampire carries his unconscious lover across the threshold of his dark domain. Ten pentagrams are engraved into the stones of the archway, signifying a mystical barrier of good fortune. The chiseled blocks form a reliable and secure structure and the sculpted bat that adorns the keystone of the arch identifies this place as the vampire's sanctum retreat.

The Ten of Pentacles signifies the reward of your labors and the total achievement of a lifetime goal. It may also denote the comforts of a stable home. You may rely upon the strength of your family and loved ones to carry you through a period of emotional or physical strain. Those closest to you will lend support when you need them most. The abundance of pentacles that adorn the sturdy arch signify wealth and stability, suggesting that you will soon enjoy a substantial monetary gain. It also signifies that your current relationship is strong and built upon a solid foundation. This emotional security contributes to the realization of a dream that you have been working toward for a long time. You have built an enduring legacy and your destiny is well within your grasp.

ARTWORK TITLE: THRESHOLD (1998)

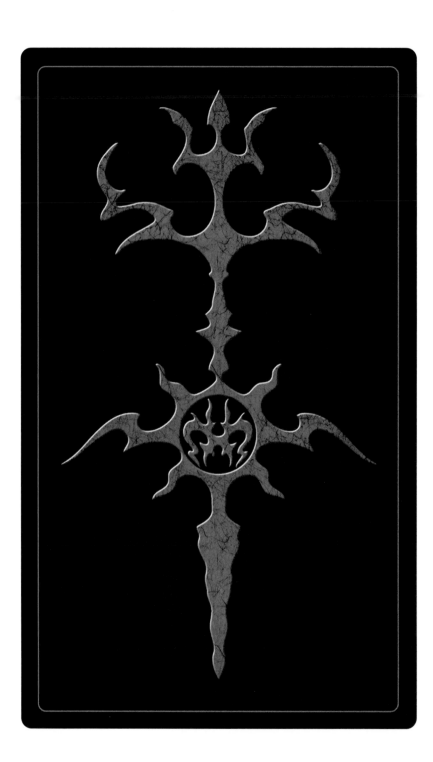

Reading The Tarot

Let the ancient art of Tarot Reading open doors, answer questions and broaden your understanding.

Tarot cards can be used to foretell future events and to enlighten the inquirer as to the best path to follow concerning matters of love, money, health and general prosperity, and offering insightful advice.

Allow your intuition to guide you as you interpret the cards. Although the cards have individual meanings, the reader should also consider the meaning of a card's position and how each card relates to the others in the spread for the most accurate reading.

If reading for another person be sure to keep them actively involved during the reading, asking or answering questions, rather than simply observing.

Decide from the following spreads which is most appropriate for the type of question you wish to ask. Shuffle the cards while thinking of the matter in question. Although the reverse meaning of each card is defined, some readers choose not to follow this method, therefore, it is not required that you reverse the cards when shuffling them. Next, cut the deck into three piles. Gather up the piles and begin laying out the cards, one at a time, in the order that they appear in the spread. Make sure the cards are dealt face-down, then after the spread is complete, turn each card over in order.

THE CELTIC CROSS

To view the past and present, to foretell future events and see the factors that influence one's life.

Select the card which best represents the person about whom the inquiry is being made. Wands represent those with yellow or red hair, and blue eyes. Cups for people with light brown hair and fair complexion. Swords for those with dark brown hair, and grey, hazel or blue eyes. Pentacles for raven-haired, dark eyed people. If the reader knows the inquirer well enough, then he/she may

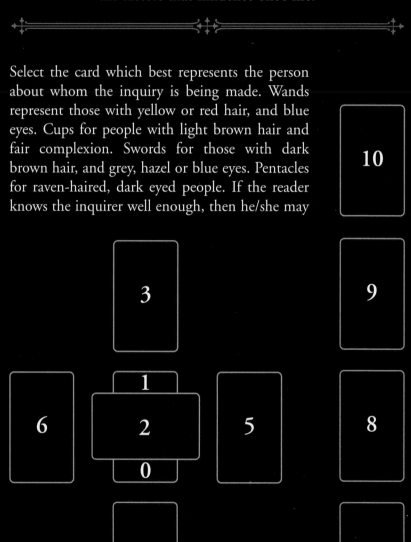

choose a signifying card based on the inquirer's character traits rather than their physical traits.

Next, the reader and the inquirer must shuffle and cut the deck three times each, then place the deck face down and lay out the cards in the order shown.

0 **Signifying Card**—This is the card chosen to represent the person about whom an inquiry is being made.

1 **Present**—This card covers the signifying card and represents present environment and influences.

2 **Obstacles**—Placed horizontally across the first, this card designates obstacles, and may represent a person or an event which is causing opposition.

3 **Future Influences**—Placed above, this card represents future influences and may include the highest state that the inquirer can achieve, the inquirer's ideal or standard of perfection, or what the inquirer ultimately wishes to attain.

4 **Past Influences**—Placed below, this card represents long held beliefs, ideals, or people from one's past, which have previously influenced one's path.

5 **Past Events**—Signifies past occurrences or that which the inquirer is moving away from.

6 **Future Influences**—Designates future influences.

7 **Attitude**—Represents the inquirer's attitude towards the matter and how the inquirer affects the world.

8 **House**—Represents the home or environment, people or events that currently influence the inquirer or hold sway over a matter..

9 **Concerns**—The inquirer's hopes and fears.

10 **Future Events**—Foretells of events on the horizon and ultimately provides insight as to the outcome of a matter.

THE MYSTIC SEVEN

For divining the answer to a specific question or
when seeking guidance in a particular matter.

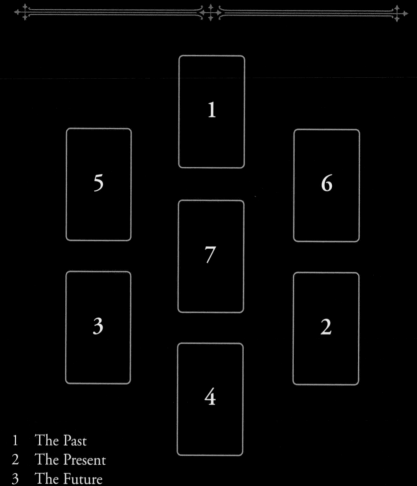

1   The Past
2   The Present
3   The Future
4   The Advised Path—what the inquirer should do to gain more
    control over the current situation.
5   Influences—the current environment and how it might affect
    the matter.
6   Obstacles—that which inhibits the inquirer.
7   The Outcome

THE VAMPIRE'S KISS

This gothic oracle enables those seeking guidance in love to determine compatibility and discover their true soulmate.

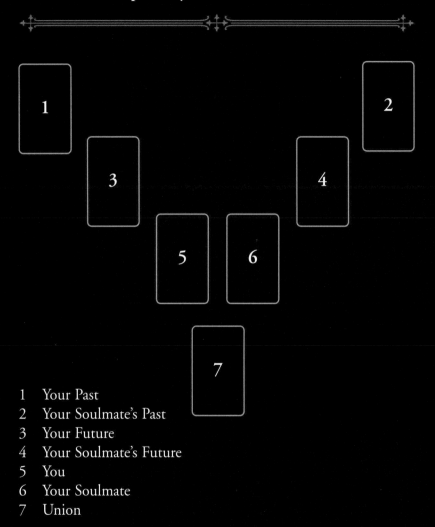

1 Your Past
2 Your Soulmate's Past
3 Your Future
4 Your Soulmate's Future
5 You
6 Your Soulmate
7 Union

The Vampire's Kiss layout is used to reveal the qualities that your designated Soulmate will possess. This spread may also be used to determine if the one you currently desire is truly compatible with you, and also to forecast the possibilities for a long-term relationship.

The Pentagram

This oracle allows us to see the influential forces of the universe that surround us at the present time.

1. You
2. Love
3. Health
4. Wealth
5. Spirit
6. The Hand of Fate

THE GOTHIC ARCH

This oracle allows us to glimpse reminders of the past in order
to glean wisdom that will guide present and future actions.

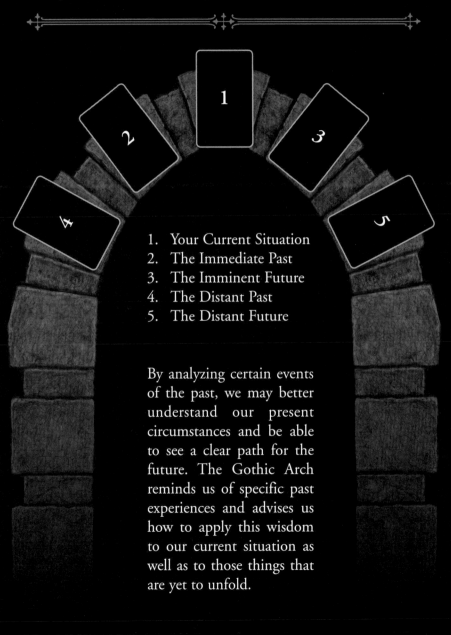

1. Your Current Situation
2. The Immediate Past
3. The Imminent Future
4. The Distant Past
5. The Distant Future

By analyzing certain events
of the past, we may better
understand our present
circumstances and be able
to see a clear path for the
future. The Gothic Arch
reminds us of specific past
experiences and advises us
how to apply this wisdom
to our current situation as
well as to those things that
are yet to unfold.

JOSEPH VARGO resides in Cleveland, Ohio where he has been conjuring fantasy artwork professionally since 1986. His gothic images open a gateway to the darkside and dare the viewer to venture within. Joseph's haunting visions of fantasy and horror have appeared in numerous publications, and his lithographs, printwear and best-selling Gothic Tarot deck are distributed worldwide. Joseph's musical project Nox Arcana explores various occult concepts, ancient mythologies and dark themes such as haunted cathedrals and mansions, the Necronomicon and the gothic realm of Transylvania. With his partner, Christine Filipak, Joseph has created and published a series of fantasy art calendars, the anthology *Tales from the Dark Tower*, the gothic periodical *Dark Realms Magazine* and the original oracle deck, *Madame Endora's Fortune Cards*. Among Vargo's numerous creative outlets, The Gothic Tarot is a crowning achievement in his impressive career.

Joseph Vargo may be reached through Monolith Graphics at:
goth@monolithgraphics.com

JOSEPH IORILLO is a freelance writer living in Cleveland Heights, Ohio. He is a *summa cum laude* graduate of John Carroll University and holds a Bachelor of Arts degree in English. Since 2000, Joseph has been a feature writer for *Dark Realms Magazine,* contributing numerous articles on topics as diverse as secret societies, ancient Sumeria, horror cinema, haunted houses and theories of the afterlife. In addition, he has contributed short stories to the anthology, *Tales From the Dark Tower,* and has written the foreward and commentary for *Born of the Night: The Gothic Fantasy Artwork of Joseph Vargo.* Mr. Iorillo has also written several contemporary mystery and suspense novels, his latest project being the psychological thriller, *This House Is Empty Now.* He holds a lifelong interest in the esoteric mysteries of the world as well as all things supernatural.

Joseph Iorillo may be reached through Monolith Graphics at:
goth@monolithgraphics.com